CREEKS & HARBOURS OF THE SOLENT

K. ADLARD COLES
REVISED BY DAVID SYLVESTER-BRADLEY

CREEKS & HARBOURS
OF THE
SOLENT
NEEDLES TO CHICHESTER

Tenth Edition

First Published   1933
Second Edition   1936
Reprinted   1939
Third Edition   1946
Fourth Edition   1948
Fifth Edition   1954
Sixth Edition   1959
Seventh Edition   1963
Eighth Edition   1972
Reprinted   1973
Ninth Edition   1981
Tenth Edition   1987

This edition published in 1987 by
Nautical Books

In imprint of Conway Maritime Press Ltd,
24 Bride Lane, Fleet Street,
London EC4 8DR

Typeset by Witwell Ltd, Liverpool
Printed and bound by R. J. Acford

Books by K. Adlard Coles

Heavy Weather Sailing
North Biscay Pilot (with A. N. Black)
Channel Harbours & Anchorages (Solent to St. Malo)
North Brittany Harbours & Anchorages (with H. G. Hasler)
Shell Pilot to the South Coast Harbours
North Atlantic
Close Hauled (Riga to Southampton)
In Broken Water (Solent to Baltic)*
In Finnish Waters*
Mary Anne among 10,000 Islands (Finland)*
Sailing Days*
More Sailing Days*
Sailing and Cruising*
Yacht Racing Rules Simplified*

These titles are at present out of print

Caution
While great care has been taken in the compilation of
this book, it is regretted that neither the authors nor the
publishers can accept responsibility for any inaccuracies or
mishaps arising from the work.

Contents

Preface to the Tenth Edition

The Creeks of the Isle of Wight by K Adlard Coles, already author of *Close Hauled* and *In Broken Water*, was published by The Yachtsman Publishing Co, Ltd in 1928 at the price of two shillings. It was followed by the first edition of *Creeks and Harbours of the Solent*, published by Edward Arnold & Co in 1933. That edition did not include Langstone or Chichester harbours, but it set a style that remained popular with yachtsmen for thirty years. Sadly, Adlard Coles has died. He was, by the end of his life, the author of some eighteen books on sailing, including such classics as *Heavy Weather Sailing* and *Channel Harbours & Anchorages*. His last work was his autobiography, *Sailing Years*. His early book, *Close Hauled* has just been issued in paperback.

Now we have the tenth edition of *Creeks and Harbours of the Solent*. It is just over fifty years since the first edition and it seems appropriate to re-print the following two paragraphs from the preface to that first edition.

'The name "The Solent" applies to the belt of sea between the mainland and the Isle of Wight. The Venerable Bede, 637-735, the first accredited recorder of written history of England, states that "The Island is situated opposite the division (Southampton Water) between the South Saxons and the Gewissoe, being separated from it by a Sea, three miles over, which is called Solente," He speaks also of the River Hamble, which he calls "Homelea" (see also Camden's *Britannia*, by William Gibson, London, 1695; also 2nd edition, 1722.)

'So again the Director-General of the Ordnance Survey: "The Solent applies to the belt of sea between Hurst Castle and the Needles to Southsea Castle and Bembridge Foreland, 'Spithead' applies to the roadstead at the eastern end of the Solent extending about two miles N.W. and S.E. along the south-west side of the Spit Sand, from Gilkicker Point to Spit Fort, with an average breadth of one and a half miles."'

Since the ninth edition was published, there have been a great many changes in the Solent yachting scene. The IALA Maritime Buoyage System 'A' is now fully established and has resulted in a few more changes, but the big difference has been in the development of marinas and especially marina-villages. For yachtsmen who like to get away from it all, there are still remote anchorages where a shoal-draft vessel can be alone; especially craft that are able to take the mud and dry out at low water. Pottering round the Solent can still be fun; the lively sailing scene, the beautiful views and serene anchorages still provide what must be one of the finest cruising grounds around the British Isles.

David Sylvester-Bradley

Acknowledgements

Most of the charts and tidal data are, as before, based on Admiralty charts, the *Channel Pilot*, and the *Pocket Tidal Stream Atlas of the Solent and Adjacent Waters* by permission of the Controller of HM Stationery Office and the Hydrographer of the Navy. I am indebted to the British Transport Docks Board for permission to base the chart of Southampton Water on their surveys. I am likewise indebted to them for the surveys on which the chart of Hamble River is based, and also to Captain J. C. Nicholl, Harbour Master, who provided the latest information used. The chart of Lymington River is based, by permission, on surveys for the Lymington Harbour Commissioners and with advice from Mr F. V. Woodford, Harbour Master.

General thanks are due to the Harbour Masters and their staffs for the assistance given in the revision necessary for this edition. In particular Captain J. Rose of Yarmouth, Mr W. H. J. Grindey of the Beaulieu River and Captain J. C. Nicholl of Hamble River.

The office of the Queen's Harbour Master Portsmouth, particularly Lieutenant Commander John Whitehouse, has been very ready with advice and information, for which I am very grateful. I have been much helped by Mr Michael Wason of Totland, Colonel David Gibson of Hamstead and Miss Sheila Cronin, Manageress of the Royal Victoria Yacht Club, Wootton. Captain Ian McKay has been unfailingly courteous and helpful through the years; indeed, I have found it always a pleasure to visit the Chichester Harbour Conservancy of which he is both Manager and Harbour Master.

Peter Bruce, the author of *Solent Harzards*, has been the source of a lot of interesting information and has helped me greatly in getting round some of the less accessible creeks in quick time. Finally, Commander Erroll Bruce has generously given of his time and great knowledge of yachting in helping me with the preparation of this edition; I owe him an immense debt from over many years.

Chichester Harbour
p.119

Langstone
Harbour p.107

Fareham
and Porchester
Lakes p.93

Portsmouth Harbour
p.85

Bembridge Harbour
p.101

S O L E N T

Cowes and Medina River
p.49

Wootton Creek
p.80

Hamble River
and Titchfield Haven p.70

Southampton Water p.56

T H E

Beaulieu River
p.41

Lymington River p.27

Newtown River
p.34

Keyhaven Lake & Achorages
p.12

Yarmouth
Harbour
p.20

Explanation of Terms and Sailing Directions

Chart Datum. The datum of the charts in this edition is approximately LAT, which for practical purposes is the lowest predicted tide, ignoring exceptional meteorological conditions. Lowering the datum to a level to which the tide rarely falls has the pessimistic result in the Solent of showing from 1½ft to 2ft (0.5 to 0.6m) less water than formerly when the chart datum was approximately at the level of MLWS (Mean Low Water Springs). Many minor creeks useful for shoal draft craft are now shown as drying out. In order to clarify the position, the tidal heights above chart datum are given at the head of each chapter and it is necessary only to add the appropriate figure to arrive at depths at MLWS and MLWN.

In the text where references are made to low water, the abbreviation CD (chart datum) is frequently added to emphasize the point that there will be more water at MLWS, which is important when calculating depths over shallows. For example, where a depth at CD on part of the Hamilton Bank off Portsmouth is given as 2ft (0.6m), reference to the tidal heights indicates that, with the addition of the appropriate 2ft at MLWS, the depth will be doubled to 4ft (1.2m) and at MLWN there will be about 7½ft (2.3m), which is a very different matter.

Metrification. Charted depths and drying heights are shown on the charts in metres to the first decimal point, but as these are direct conversions from the nearest foot they remain approximate only. In the text both feet and metres are given. Distances are expressed in nautical miles and cables.

Beacons and Piles. These are shown either as a small round O, or symbolized as also are perches, but the latter have been omitted where the scale is too small.

Bearings. The bearings in degrees are true, but approximate bearings are expressed in magnetic points of the compass. Local variation in 1980 is about 7°W. The terms 'port' and 'starboard' refer to the side on which objects lie when the vessel is approaching from seaward.

Abbreviations.

EC	Early Closing	Fl	Flashing	Oc	Occulting
CD	Chart Datum	G	Green	PO	Post Office
HW	High Water	Gp	Group	Q	Quick
LW	Low Water	H, horiz	Horizontal	R	Red
LAT	Lowest Astronomical Tide	h, m	Hours, minutes	S	Stripes
MHWS	Mean High Water Springs	IoW	Isle of Wight	s, sec	seconds
MHWN	Mean High Water Neaps	IQ	Interrupted Quick	SC	Sailing Club
MLWS	Mean Low Water Springs	Iso	Isophase	VQ	Very Quick
MLWN	Mean Low Water Neaps	IVQ	Interrupted Very Quick	V, vert	Vertical
B	Black	L Fl	Long Flashing	W	White
Bn	Beacon	M	Miles	Y	Yellow
Cheq	Chequered	m	metres	YC	Yacht Club
Dn	Dophin	Mag	Magnetic		
F	Fixed	NB	Notice Board		

Sailing Directions. Whilst great care has been taken that the sailing directions and the charts in this book should be accurate, the publishers and the author cannot accept any responsibility for any errors or omissions which may have escaped notice. The author would be glad to receive any information or suggestions relating to the areas covered by this book which readers may consider would improve the book. Letters should be addressed to the author at Nautical Books, A & C Black Ltd., Howard Road, Eaton Socon, Huntingdon, Cambs, PE19 3EZ.

The charts in this book are based on Admiralty charts and other authorities, by kind permission. They have been enlarged, altered and amplified to embody much information obtained by the author and other yachtsmen for the areas covered. It cannot, however, be too firmly emphasized that these charts are intended to supplement, and not to supersede, ordinary navigation charts. Admiralty charts are constantly being corrected, whereas corrections in a work of this kind can be made only on the occasion of a new edition. The following Admiralty charts will be useful to yachtsmen and others cruising in Solent waters:

No. 2045 *Outer Approaches to the Solent*
No. 2219 *Western Approaches to Solent*
No. 2040 *Solent (western part)*
No. 2793 *Cowes Harbour and River Medina*
No. 1905 *Southampton Water and Approaches*
No. 2041 *Port of Southampton*
No. 394 *Solent (eastern part)*
No. 2625 *Approaches to Portsmouth*
No. 2631 *Portsmouth Harbour*
No. 2050 *Eastern Approaches to the Solent*
No. 2022 *Harbours and Anchorages in the East Solent Area*
No. 3418 *Langstone and Chichester harbours*

Messrs Imray, Laurie, Norie & Wilson Ltd publish excellent yachtsmen's charts including all sections of the Solent, and there is a useful general coloured chart No. 11 of the whole area published by Messrs Edward Stanford Ltd.

With the information in this book, suitable coastal charts, corrected to date, and a good Nautical Almanac such as *Reed's Nautical Almanac*, a complete stranger should have no difficulty in keeping up to date with Solent navigation.

Chart Convention

Areas of water over 6ft (1.8m) in charted depth are left white, as also are marinas with varying depths. Areas of 6ft at the new chart datum and below are blue, bounded by a dotted line. This line is drawn at the equivalent of 7½ to 8ft (according to the position) at MLWS, which was the approximate chart datum in previous editions. Drying areas at CD are stippled over the colour and bounded by a solid line. In some parts the edges of the channel are so steep that the 6ft line and the drying line are so close that only the drying line can be shown on small scale.

High Water. Where there is double high water, as at Southampton at spring tides, constants on Portsmouth are given for both first and second high water. At other harbours, where there is a long stand of about 2 hours near high water, the constants are for mean HW.

Lights. Lights indicated by stars without legends or with incomplete legends represent two fixed lights arranged vertically and seen Red to port - Green to starboard, proceeding up-stream.

Channel Marking. It is a feature of many creeks described in this book that the course of the channel changes from year to year and the buoyage and leading marks are altered to suit. Thus their positions shown on the chartlets should be taken as approximate.

1 Keyhaven Lake and Anchorages

Double High Water: At Hurst, Springs - 1 h 10 m, and + 0 h 45 m Portsmouth. Neaps mean - 0 h 5 m.
Tidal Heights above datum: (at Hurst) MHWS 9 ft (2.7 m) MLWS 1.6 ft (0.5 m) MHWN 7.6 ft (2.3 m) MLWN 4.2 ft (1.3 m).
Stream sets outside off Hurst to the westward about - 1 h 10 m Portsmouth, and eastward + 4 h 45 m.
Depths above datum: Bar practically dries out. Over 2 fathoms (3.6 m) off the Camber, gradually decreasing to 5 ft (1.5 m) off Mount Lake and to a few inches (0.2 m) off the quay.
Yacht Clubs: Keyhaven Yacht Club, Hurst Castle Sailing Club.

KEYHAVEN, ON THE MAINLAND shore, is the most westerly of the Solent creeks. It lies behind Hurst Castle, which dominates the narrows of the Needles Channel. Before being taken to the scaffold, King Charles I was imprisoned here in a grim dungeon in the old round castle, but the rest of the building dates only from Victorian times and consists of flat masonry relieved by the red low and the white high lighthouses.

From Hurst to the mainland there is a mile of narrow, high beach which provides a natural breakwater against the prevailing winds to protect the entrance and 'Lake', or creek, which winds its way through the marram grass-covered marshes to Keyhaven. This peaceful harbour has changed little, apart from the greatly increased membership of the clubs and the demand for every possible mooring site. It is a friendly centre for small cruising yachts and keen sailors.

North Channel and Shingles

When sailing to the Solent from the west to Keyhaven, the North Channel may be better than the Needles Channel and is considered safer in gales. Coming from the westward a yacht should be steered with Hurst High Light bearing 097° until the North Head G buoy (*Fl (3) G 10s*) is sighted. Then steer to leave it to starboard and round into the channel running SE parallel with Hurst Beach. This gives about 10 ft (3.0 m) at CD.

If a leading line is desired it is the right extreme of Golden Hill Fort 118° in line with Brambles Chine. The latter is on the middle of the coast of Colwell Bay and the fort (with flagstaff) is at the summit of the hill ½ mile inland.

A useful lead in good weather, if wishing to take the short cut across the neck of the Shingle Bank between the North Head and the main part of the bank, is to keep Hurst Castle open its own width to the *left* of Sconce Point. This gives 10 ft (3.0 m) at low water *neap* tides, or 6½ ft (2.0 m) at MLWS but should be regarded with caution, as the Shingle Banks are apt to shoal or shift and the channel is narrow. The lead, incidentally, is on the direct course from Hurst to Poole Bar buoy.

Low Light   Round Fort   High Light

1.1. Hurst Castle from the South. 'The Trap' extends approximately three quarters of a cable south from the round fort, almost directly towards the camera.

Approach, Entrance and Channel

Approaching Hurst from the westward avoid 'The Trap', a shingle bank extending three-quarters of a cable S(Mag) from the Round Fort with little water over it at chart datum. It is in the form of a gravel projection from the beach, steep on each side. Once round the 'Trap' and Hurst Point it is possible to sail NE close inshore as far as the High Lighthouse and the old pier. Here the tidal streams vary and there is an eddy close inshore. Northward of the pier the shore is more shelving and shallow water extends seawards for a considerable distance off the cottages, and develops into a wide bar across the entrance to the river. The approach is sheltered from SW through west to north, but exposed to the east, and strangers should not attempt entry in strong winds from this direction.

Make good a position about 3 cables NE of Hurst High Light when the leading marks will be seen. These consist of a front (lower) post, and a rear (higher) post both of which carry crosses (see photograph on page 16). They are situated well up on the flats. Their position is altered from time to time to suit changes in the course of the channel, but in 1986 gave a transit of 305 mag. Bring the marks into line and steer on their transit. The bar nearly dries out at chart datum but about 2ft (0.6m) can be expected at MLWS and there is said to be over 4ft (1.2m) at MLWN.

The feature of the entry to the river is the North Point of the sand and shingle promontory extending in a NNW direction for nearly ½ mile from Hurst Point, not to be confused with the long Hurst Beach to Milford-on-Sea. For some years North Point has been moving eastward and there now is a constriction of the current between the point and the mud bank.

13

Keyhaven Lake: Soundings in metres. Add 0.5 m (1.6 ft) at MLWS, 1.3 m (4.2 ft) at MLWN. Based on British Admiral Chart No. 2219, with the permission of HM Stationery Office and of the Hydrographer of the Navy.

1.2.   The anchorage east of Hurst Castle.

As a result the channel round North Point is well scoured, the deep water being close in. Continue on the transit of the leading marks until a pair of buoys R and G will be seen marking the entrance. The channel is then clearly indicated by G starboard hand buoys. Steer to pass about 30ft (9m) off the extremity of North Point leaving another green buoy to starboard. This is the narrowest part of the channel and there is only about 50ft (15m) between the point and the buoy. Follow the shingle point round (once round it the channel quickly deepens to over 2 fathoms (3.6m)) leaving a further green buoy to starboard. The channel then leads about WSW and the stream, which may be strong off the point, weakens.

Approaching from the eastward it is merely necessary to keep in sufficient depth of water, steering for the High Light and pier, until on the transit of the leading marks, when proceed as before. The stream along the Hampshire coast is much weaker inshore where it pays to cheat a foul tide, but give the sewer outfall beacons a berth of ¼ mile at low water, and note that there is an obstruction and shoal SE of the entrance to Hawker's Lake.

After entering Keyhaven Lake at North Point a misleadingly wide expanse of water will be seen ahead if it is near high water. The lake on the port hand is the Camber, but at low tide most of this dries out leaving only a short creek leading to a dilapidated private landing stage and a longer creek marked by three black and white perches beyond it, 2ft (0.6m) at LW Neaps, which winds its way through the mud to a quay near Hurst Castle. Likewise there will be a camber seen ahead north of Rabbit Point, leading westerly to Hurst beach, but this also dries out, although a few light draft yachts are moored near its entrance.

1.3. The leading marks at the entrance to Keyhaven River 1986.

1.4. The pair of buoys at the entrance to Keyhaven River.

The picture at low water would be very different as the navigable river is then comparatively narrow. It bends round a semi-circle of gently sloping mud bank (much of which is covered at HW) from SW through west and NW almost to north. The bend in the channel is well marked by three more green buoys on the starboard side. The position of the buoys is varied from time to time and may differ from that shown on the chartlet. The channel is at least 7ft (2.1m) deep as far as Mount Lake, which branches off to the westward towards Hurst Beach. Above Mount Lake the river narrows and the depth falls to 5ft and 4ft (1.5m and 1.2m) for 2 cables and then to 3ft (0.9m) before the last reach, which practically dries out. The line of moorings in the centre of the river shows the direction of the channel very clearly but if the wind is blowing the yachts broadside across the fairway, steer across their bows rather than under their sterns which may be close to the mud. In the upper reach there are two lines of small craft and the best water is between them close to the port hand line leaving a trot of power craft close to port. When the old quay is abeam, keep to port close to the stakes which remain from an ancient quay and inside a line of fishing craft.

Mount Lake has 4ft (1.2m) at CD for over a cable from its entrance and is navigable for most of its length with sufficient rise of tide, but strangers may not find the best water as in the channel this is only about 40ft (12m) wide.

Lights: Keyhaven Lake has no lights, but entrance is possible if it is not too dark to identify North Point and craft moored in the river.

Moorings, Anchorage and Facilities

Moorings are laid almost everywhere from the Camber to Keyhaven and in Mount Lake. Even in Hawker's Lake there are moorings for shallow draft yachts which can dry out. Moorings should not be picked up without local advice as the owners usually return in the evenings. The only position left for anchoring is just within the entrance WSW of North point, where the water is deep but there is room only for a few yachts. The position can be uncomfortable in strong SW winds and it is best to moor with two anchors which should be buoyed. Telegraph cables cross the river twice at the bend between the Camber and Mount Lake and are also laid on the river bed farther up, where if anchoring temporarily in an emergency be sure to use a really strong tripping line.

There is anchorage outside off the mud flats in NW winds but the popular one is under the lee of the shingle bank between the old pier near the High Light and the cottages just north of it, where the water begins to shoal and anchorage is necessarily farther out. The anchorage is sheltered from SW, W and NW winds but suffers from the swell of passing ships. It is used principally in day time when as many as twenty or more yachts bring up on a summer afternoon, and use dinghies to land on the shingle or to proceed up the river to Keyhaven. During gales the anchorage is uncomfortable owing to tidal eddies but it provides tolerable shelter in good holding ground and may be useful if arriving at night when the tide is turning foul in the Solent.

At Keyhaven there is a poor public landing on steps at the end of the old quay and a new quay beyond the yacht clubs with dinghy landing at the hard adjacent to it. The River Warden (Mr Tom Holt) has a new office between the Keyhaven Yacht Club and the New Quay. Near The Keyhaven Yacht Club (with its private dinghy pontoon) and the Hurst Castle Sailing Club, there is the yacht yard of the West Solent Boat Builders who undertake laying-up and repairs and provide fuel and water for yachts. At the hard, where there is 6ft (1.8m) at HW Springs, yachts can be scrubbed, and there is a launching site for dinghies, though it is often congested in the season, particularly at week-ends. Behind the Keyhaven Yacht Club there is a car park and the Gun Inn is just across the road. Buses very occasionally run to Milford-on-Sea, a mile distant, where there are the usual facilities of a small town (EC Wednesday). In summer there are motor launches from the quay to Hurst Castle, which is maintained by the Ministry of Works and is open to the public.

1.5.   The River Warden's office and the hard at the new quay.

1.6. View from the hard at low water showing the channel between the fishing craft and the wall.

1.7. The old life-boat house at Totland Bay.

Nearby Anchorages

Yarmouth Roads is the nearest anchorage to Hurst Road – see Yarmouth – but there are two interesting ones in the Needles Channel. The nearest is Totland Bay (distance only 1½ miles from Hurst) which is sheltered in southerly and easterly winds. If draft allows, anchor close inshore between the pier and the old life-boat house, where there is good holding ground in sand and mud. Further out there is a heavy growth of weed and holding is less sure. The light at the pier head enables the anchorage to be used at night under suitable conditions. There are shops at Totland.

Alum Bay, over a mile farther towards the Needles, is famous for its multi-coloured cliffs at the foot of which there are sands suitable for children. There is a cliff path and chair-lift leading to large motor coach and car parks, and a café. Nowadays there may be many yachts in the bay on a summer's day. The anchorage is good in southerly and easterly winds, though during gales squalls come down from the cliffs above. If sheltering in a southerly gale be prepared to leave quickly in the event of the wind veering later towards NW, as this may put the yacht on a lee shore. The anchorage is little used at night but the Shingles buoys are an aid to navigation. The best position is off the ruins of the pier, of which only one pile and an inner pair remain standing. Less than a cable to the northward of the approach is the Five Finger Rock 2ft (0.6m) CD, and to the southward the Long Rock. Long Rock is in two parts, the inshore section of which dries out about 2ft (0.6m) CD and is often marked by a lobster-pot buoy. The westerly section is awash at CD and difficult to find. Together they are a danger to craft leaving an inshore anchorage and proceeding direct to the Needles. Both Five Finger and Long Rock can be avoided by keeping Warden Fort open of Hatherwood Point until what is left of the ruined pier bears East (mag), then sail in to the required depth of water – see chart. Owners familiar with Alum Bay may pass between the ledges off Hatherwood Point and Five Finger Rock.

Alum Bay: Based on British Admiralty Chart No. 2219, with the permission of HM Stationery Office and the Hydrographer of the Navy.

2 Yarmouth Harbour

Double High Water: Springs — 1h 5m and + 0h 50m. Portsmouth. Neaps mean + 0h 5m.
Tidal Heights above datum: MHWS 10.1ft (3.1m) MLWS 1.9ft (0.6m) MHWN 8.3ft (2.5m) MLWN 4.6ft (1.4m).
Stream sets outside strongly to the westward — 1h 15m Portsmouth and to the eastward + 4h 50m.
Depths above datum: 7ft (2.1m) in the approach channel and about 6ft (1.8m) in the harbour itself.
Yacht Clubs: Royal Solent Yacht Club. Yarmouth Sailing Club.

YARMOUTH IS UNDOUBTEDLY the most popular of the Solent harbours for visiting yachts, being at a convenient distance from most centres in the Solent and providing good deep water berths. The harbour is very well run for yachtsmen and provides the best port of departure if bound west or to France.

The town itself has a mellow charm and the castle at the harbour entrance lends a mediaeval appearance as viewed from the sea.

In the Middle Ages Yarmouth and its harbour provided the first objective for attack by any French squadrons entering the Solent. It was not until the castle was built for its defence in 1537 that the town really began to prosper and grow. This massive building still remains in good condition and is preserved as an ancient monument. Behind the castle stands what was once the house of the Governor of the Island, where Charles II made a short stay while on a visit to Hurst. It is now the George Hotel, much frequented by yachtsmen.

At high water a dinghy can proceed up the River Yar and along the winding creek nearly to Freshwater. The surrounding woods, the reeds and pools backed by hills make this a pleasant trip. There are coastal walks from Yarmouth in the direction of the Needles and eastwards to Newtown. The harbour is a good place for children as there are always people about, and there is bathing from the beach to the westward.

The Approach and Entrance

Approaching from the west there are two things to consider. In deep water by the Black Rock buoy some three-quarters of a mile to the west of the entrance there is Fiddler's Race, a genuine small scale race, that can be dangerous for dinghies and unpleasant for yachts of small size; and farther inshore lies the rock itself which dries 2ft (0.6m) at low tide. Small craft can pass inside the rock, thus avoiding the race, by keeping the end of the pier, a cable east of Sconce Point, in line with Hurst Castle; this course is said to allow 2ft (0.6m) at MLWS, but almost dries out at chart datum.

The approach from the east is easy, and it is only necessary to make allowance for the

2.1. The entrance to Yarmouth.

strong tidal streams. By keeping on a course a little outside the end of the pier there is ample water for any yacht. Small craft can keep farther inshore to cheat the tide, except at low water, when there is very little depth inside the pier end of the east side.

Make a position about ¼ cable west of the end of Yarmouth Pier and bring the leading marks (black and white diamonds on posts set behind the quay) into line at 187°. Steer on or close to this transit, but avoid being set too far eastward of it by wind or tide or when tacking. The channel narrows as the entrance is approached but carries 7ft (2.1m) as far as the ferry jetty and 6ft (1.8m) beyond it. Course should be altered to leave the jetty and ramp to port.

When the ferry ramp comes abeam to port, the main channel turns to the west parallel with the inside of the breakwater, leaving the A line of mooring piles for larger yachts to starboard and the B line to port. In addition, there are three lines of mooring piles for smaller yachts with narrow fairways between them. Incoming yachts should have warps and fenders ready and are usually hailed from a boat by one of the Berthing Masters giving berthing instructions. If the Berthing Master or his Deputy is not immediately available it is best to berth temporarily at the Town Quay and await directions, as anchoring is prohibited.

21

Yarmouth Harbour: Soundings in metres. Add 0.6 m (1.9 ft) at MLWS, 1.4 m (4.6 ft) at MLWN. Based on British Admiralty Chart No. 2040, with the permission of HM Stationery Office and of the Hydrographer of the Navy.

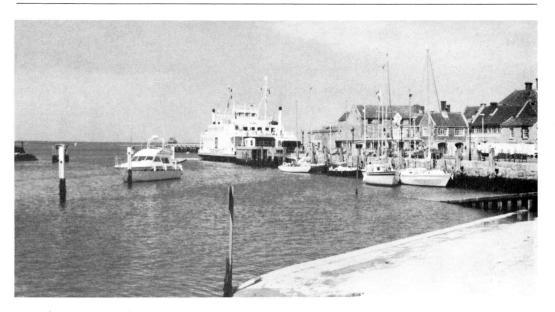

2.2   The temporary berths at Town Quay.

Within the harbour there is not a great range of tide, only about 8ft (2.4m) on ordinary spring tides, but the stream can be quite strong, especially on the ebb. There is then little room for tacking in the narrow fairway, especially if other craft or dinghies are under way, unless the yacht is small or very handy. Auxiliary power is usually used. Motor yachts must proceed at reduced speed. Depths vary within the harbour which tends to silt but is dredged area by area during the winter. It is best to regard the whole harbour as about 6ft (1.8m). There are three tide gauges, one on the pier, another on the ferry jetty for incoming vessels, and one facing south on the dolphin opposite for vessels leaving the harbour.

Entry Prohibited: When the harbour is full a red flag is hoisted at a flagpole at the seaward end of the ferry jetty and a "HARBOUR FULL" sign may be displayed (a R light at night). Yarmouth is so popular that the harbour is usually full by 5pm on Saturdays in summer although, in the event of a yacht leaving, the Harbour Master may authorize a small yacht to enter and occupy the vacant berth.

Lights: There are two fixed green lights on the leading marks. The end of the pier outside the harbour is marked by two fixed red lights and in fog two white lights are shown as well. The end of the ferry jetty is marked by two fixed red lights and in fog a fixed yellow light. At the far end of the quay there is a fixed white light facing the harbour, showing red towards the quay itself. There are also two vertical red lights on the end of the groyne at the west end of the harbour and a floodlit pontoon providing the Pilot Boat berth.

2.3.   South Quay with the Harbour Office and fuelling station.

Moorings, Anchorages and Facilities

The harbour comes under the authority of the Yarmouth Harbour Commissioners, whose powers were widened under an Act of Parliament to include the approach, the pier and water adjacent to it, and also the River Yar above the bridge. The speed limit is 4 knots.

Yarmouth is a natural yacht harbour but the dredging in 1958, and the South Quay which followed, enclosed some 70 acres accommodating about 300 yachts, and more at times. The development was an example of enterprise long before the creation of any marinas in this country. Dredging and improvements have continued and the harbour is a model for good relations between the controlling authority and the yachtsmen using it. Harbour dues are reasonable and special annual terms can be arranged.

Yachts berth fore and aft to the piles of which there are five lines, A, B, C, D and E and the piles on each line are numbered from the entrance. The berth between No 5 and 6 E piles is allotted to the lifeboat. Care must be taken always to moor to the piles and not to other yachts, apart from breast ropes or temporarily on arrival or departure. At the west end of the harbour there are also berths for a few small craft to moor bows to piles and sterns to the groyne.

When the harbour is full, anchorage may be found outside; large yachts usually bringing up to the west of the pierhead clear of the entrance channel and to the south of the big ship moorings, and smaller ones farther inshore according to their draft and the tidal conditions.

2.4. Looking up the River Yar from the swing bridge.

This anchorage is reasonable in offshore winds or in settled weather, but the streams are strong so it is best to anchor as close inshore as safety permits. The anchorage is exposed to all northerly winds and it is said that in the gale of 1876 a ketch of 6ft (1.8m) draft, anchored in the roads, was swept by huge seas right over the breakwater, which presumably was then lower than it is today. In northerly gales and on a big spring tide even the harbour itself can be uncomfortable near high water.

On the east side of the pier there are private moorings for small craft but room can usually be found for yachts of light draft to anchor in settled weather. This position gets some protection by the pier from the prevailing winds and is convenient for the club and the town. Whether anchoring to the west or east of the pier there is often a roll, even if only from passing ships.

If a prolonged stay is intended, the Harbour Master should be consulted. The Harbour Master and Secretary to the Harbour Commissioners is Captain J. M. Rose. His Deputy and Treasurer to the Commissioners is Mr A. Bolton. They have an office near the Town Quay (Tel: IoW 760321). The duty Berthing Master may be found at the Harbour Office on South Quay (Tel: 760300).

The swing bridge over the R Yar opens at times set by the Harbour Master and displayed on the Harbour Office notice board. A new swing bridge is (1986) under construction just south of the present one. It is expected to be opened in the summer of 1987.

Landing in Yarmouth Harbour is easy as there are several slips and pontoons. There is a crane, fuel pumps, water, a marine engineer's workshop (where batteries can be charged), slipway and dinghy compound at the South Quay. This extends the whole length of the bridge road between the training groyne and the town. Yachts may go alongside for petrol, water, etc. At the time of writing the depth is 8ft (2.4m) but it is safer to take it as 6ft (1.8m). There are two scrubbing berths on piles near the breakwater for yachts up to 6ft (1.8m) draft on application to the Harbour Master.

The town of Yarmouth itself is well adapted to the needs of yachtsmen. The Royal Solent YC is a leading and hospitable yacht club and the Yarmouth SC has been re-established; two hotels (the George and the Bugle), the Wheatsheaf restaurant and other inns and small restaurants add to the facilities. Customs formalities are quick as their office (Quay Street) is open from 6am to 10pm in summer months. The PO is in Quay St, next to Holding's booksellers, stationers and newsagents (including Sunday papers), and there are small shops of all kinds, EC Wednesday. There are three yacht yards: Harold Hayles (Yarmouth IW) Ltd, just west of the bridge, and above the bridge the River Yar Boat Yard which lays up many yachts. Launching sites from dinghy slips at the quays or from the ferry slip by arrangement with Harbour Master. Car park adjacent. The lifeboat is famous for her work in the Needles Channel and south of the Island. Frequent ferries run to Lymington and in the summer there are occasional excursion steamers to Bournemouth and elsewhere. Sand Hard Ferries provide a useful local service to the bathing beach and to yachts. There are good bus connections.

3 Lymington River

Double High Water: Springs — 0h 55m and + 0h 45m Portsmouth; Neaps mean + 0h 5m.
Tidal Heights above datum: MHWS 10ft (3.0m) MLWS 1.6ft (0.45m) MHWN 8.4ft (2.6m) MLWN 4.4ft (1.3m).
Stream sets to the westward off Lymington Spit about — 1h 15m Portsmouth, and eastward + 4h 50m.
Depths: There is a minimum depth of 6ft (1.8m) in mid-channel from the river entrance to the pier railway station and Berthon Boat Co Ltd, gradually shoaling towards the channel margins. From the Berthon to the Town Quay and bridge there is a least depth of 3½ft (1.1m). The width of the channel above Harper's Post is restored by dredging from time to time.
Yacht Clubs: Royal Lymington Yacht Club, Lymington Town Sailing Club.

THE CHANNEL WINDS its way through marshes to Lymington, the old world town whose history from far into the past has been associated with ships and the sea. At one time it was an important local centre of salt and iron-smelting industries, the ironstone being quarried at Hengistbury and brought to Lymington by sea in barges and beaten out by great hammers worked by water wheel from the 'hammer ponds', of which Sowley is one. 'Jack in the Basket', the beacon with a barrel top in the approach to Lymington, used to be taken as a point of departure for ships, and it was from here that HMS *Pandora* sailed in 1790 to search the Pacific for the mutineers from the *Bounty*.

Today the river is little used for commercial purposes other than by the car ferries to Yarmouth, but it has grown to be an important yachting centre with two of the leading marinas in the Solent and many river moorings. The river is deep enough for most yachts except very deep draft craft at extreme LW springs and the yachting facilities are excellent. The town itself has grown but it retains its character and much of its old-world charm.

The Approach, Entrance and River
When entering the river the best water will be found by leaving Jack in the Basket about 150ft to port to clear Cross Boom (next port hand pile) by approximately 120ft to port. Thereafter the river is well marked by red piles with can type topmarks on the port hand and by green piles with green triangular topmarks to starboard. The deepest part of the fairway in cross-section is about in the middle third as the channel tends to shoal toward the sides. The beacons should be given a wide berth as many of them are on the mud or in very shallow water. The line of yachts on moorings near the mud on the west side of the river provide an additional aid to pilotage. Two leading posts, with red and white horizontal stripes, are erected on the flats to the south of Seymore's Post to provide a transit for the outgoing ferries and another pair, with black and white horizontal stripes, on the flats on the east side of the river south of the Cage Boom for the incoming ferry transit.

The car ferries are the only features disconcerting to the stranger. These are handled with

3.1.   The entrance showing from right to left the R. Lym YC starting platform and the first starboard hand mark.

3.2.   The ferry leading marks B and W just south of Cage Boom pile on the east side of the river.

3.3.   Harpers Post at the entrance to Lymington Yacht Haven.

3.4. Horn Reach from the roof of the R.Lym YC showing the Harbour Master's pontoon, looking south.

care but are big for the river and should not be passed too closely, especially by dinghies, owing to the suction they cause in the restricted water. The ferries have right of way and can be quite a problem at low water if several yachts are in the vicinity at the same time.

Horn Reach is the last reach up to the pier railway station and the narrowest. Harper's Post, now an east cardinal mark, indicates the spit of mud that divides the entrance to the Lymington Yacht Haven from Horn Reach, which leads past the Harbour Master's pontoon, the launching slip and the Royal Lymington Yacht Club's pontoon off which local racing classes are moored. Beyond these, also on the port hand, lies the Lymington Marina, and the main channel leads between the marina and the pier ferry terminal and station. It then bends round the end of the marina, leaving a short line of mooring piles to port and a longer line of piles to starboard, and turns to the west towards the Berthon Boat Co Ltd, leaving a wide expanse of mud on the starboard hand. This part of the channel above the ferry terminal is slightly narrower due principally to the craft moored on piles on either side. Subject to silting it carries 6ft (1.8m) as far as the yacht yard, and 3½ft (0.9m) beyond it. Finally, after passing the yacht yard, there is a short reach up to the railway bridge, leaving the Town Quay on the port side.

Lights: There are two fixed red lights near the yacht club which lead up the first reach at 320° up to Seymore's Post. The river is marked on the port side by four Fl R lights and Harper's Post Q (3) 10s. On the starboard hand there are seven Fl G lights.

Lymington River: Soundings in metres. Add 0.5m (1.6ft) at MLWS, 1.3m (4.4ft) at MLWN. Based on surveys by permission of Lymington Harbour Commissioners. Approaches based on British Admiralty Chart No. 2040, with the permission of HM Stationery Office and of the Hydrographer of the Navy.

3.5.   The R.Lym YC, it's pontoon and the lines of moorings upstream of it.

Moorings, Anchorage and Facilities
Anchorage is prohibited in the river, which is fully occupied by moorings controlled by the Harbour Commissioners and mostly rented annually, but anchorage can be found outside off the mud flats in offshore winds. The principal centre in the river is the marina of the Berthon Boat Company which is situated on the west side of the river and has 240 berths. Most of the berths are rented in advance for the season but visitors can usually be temporarily accommodated, preferably by telephoning in advance. There is also the Lymington Yacht Haven marina in Harper's Lake which has 450 berths.

The Harbour Master (Mr. F. V. Woodford, Tel: Lymington 72014) will advise on use of the Town Quay and moorings in the river. His office is near to the R Lymington YC. An area has been dredged on the opposite side of the river to the Town Quay where moorings with white buoys have been laid for visiting yachts. At the Custom's House Quay (just downstream of the Town Quay) there are pontoons where yachts can bring up six abreast. Altogether there are now berths for about 100 visiting yachts, apart from the marinas. Yachts up to 6ft (1.8m) draft may be scrubbed at the Town Slip, but the time must be arranged with the Harbour Master. Car park, water and public lavatories are adjacent and also the Ship Hotel and restaurant, chandlers and nearby in Quay Hill a good shop for yachting clothes and oilskins.

The largest yacht yard is the Berthon Boat Co Ltd, just north of their marina, which has craftsmen for all kinds of repairs and yacht building, including ocean racers and has a

3.6.   The ferry terminal on the right, Lymington Marina on the left and the channel between.

3.7.   The Town Quay with visitors pontoon and the Berthon Boat Co Ltd in the background.

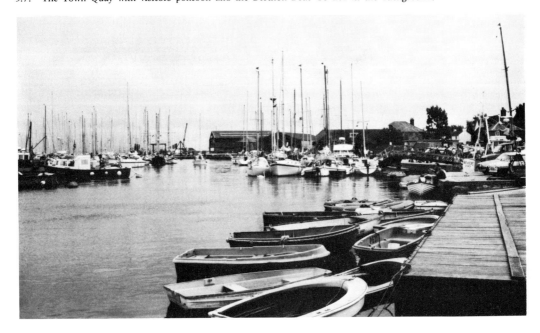

chandlery and garage. The customs office, with 24 hours service, is situated with the Harbour Master in a three story building between R Lym YC and the Lym Town SC. The Lymington Yacht Haven at Waterford has an extensive chandlery. In Mill Lane, at the bottom of Station Street and not a long walk away, there are Aquaboats, who can undertake yacht repairs and laying up, and Mr Bill Smith with his facilities for repairs, laying up and boat transport. Laurent Giles and Partners, the yacht designers and agents, are in Quay Hill, while Hoods, sailmakers, and Brookes & Gatehouse, electronic instrument makers, are close to the Berthon Boat Co Ltd. In addition, there are several smaller firms supplying yachting requirements such as sails, clothing and chandlery.

The R Lymington YC and the Lymington Town SC are at Waterford where there are car parks adjacent to the clubs and a small general stores with an off licence (closed on Thursdays, but open Sundays) which also sells newspapers. A Sub-Post Office (also grocers, EC Wednesdays) is in Westfield Road 200 yards west of Bath Road.

Water can be had at the marina pontoons, at the Town Quay and the Bath Road public pontoon and at yacht yards; fuel at the Marina pontoons and yacht yards; launching sites at public slipway adjacent to yacht clubs or at the Town Quay.

The main shopping centre is in the High Street, which despite the addition of a few multiple shops has changed little over the centuries, and leads up the hill from Quay Street to St Thomas' church. Here will be found banks and good individual shops of every description, including a leading bookshop. EC Wednesday. There are also hotels: Angel, Stanwell House and others; restaurants and garages and good travel agents. Communications are excellent: from pier and town stations to Brockenhurst linking up with fast electric trains (Waterloo, Southampton, Bournemouth and Weymouth), buses to all parts and frequent car ferries to Yarmouth, IOW. The New Forest, with its lovely countryside is within easy reach.

4 Newtown River

Double High Water: Springs about — 1h 0m and + 0h 50m Portsmouth; Neaps mean — 0h 5m.
Tidal Heights above datum at Solent Banks: MHWS 11.2ft (3.4m) MLWS 1.6ft (0.5m) MHWN 9.2ft (2.8m) MLWN 4.8ft (1.5m).
Stream sets outside to the westward — 1h 15m Portsmouth, and to the eastward + 4h 45m.
Depths: About 3ft (0.9m) on the bar; 5ft (1.5m) to 11ft (3.3m) in channel as far as Fishhouse Pt 4ft (1.2m) with deeper pools within, falling to 3ft (0.9m) at junction with Causeway Lake and shallow beyond.

THERE MUST BE few yachtsmen who, after visiting Newtown for the first time, have not returned to it again year after year. The snug anchorage, the creeks winding silently through the marshes and the unspoilt countryside, combine to give the place a character of its own. Perhaps the finger-prints of history linger on in some distant way to the present time.

Newtown, under its original name of Francheville, was once the capital of the Isle of Wight and a flourishing seaport. In 1377 the town was sacked and burnt by the French. When partially rebuilt, the name was changed to Newtown, but it was too vulnerable to attack from the sea for its former prosperity to be regained. However, from 1585 to 1832 it returned two members of Parliament, which included John Churchill, later Duke of Marlborough. The old town hall has been skilfully restored and maintained in perfect repair by the National Trust, and is well worth visiting. There are still lanes and cuttings through the trees that once were busy streets some 600 years ago.

The village now consists only of a church and a few houses and cottages. There are no ships in the river but many yachts, so many in fact that it is preferable if possible to avoid a visit on August week-ends and bank holidays.

The Approaches and Creeks

Newtown River lies on the Island shore, 3½ miles east of Yarmouth and seven cables ESE of Hamstead Ledge. The best time for a first visit is on a rising tide before the mud flats are covered and the trend of the channels can still be seen. At high water everything is covered and strangers often go aground despite the perches marking the mud.

Approaching from the west make Hamstead Ledge green conical buoy. Here the stream is very strong and the water rough if the wind is contrary to it. In good weather the buoy can be passed on the wrong side, leaving it a cable to port and crossing the ledges in over 3 fathoms. Then steer due east for ½ mile, when the small red spherical bar buoy will be close at hand.

From the eastward keep Yarmouth Pier well open of Hamstead Point to avoid Newtown Gravel Banks and leave the bar buoy to port. The entrance to the River and the leading marks

Leading Marks   Fishhouse Pt.

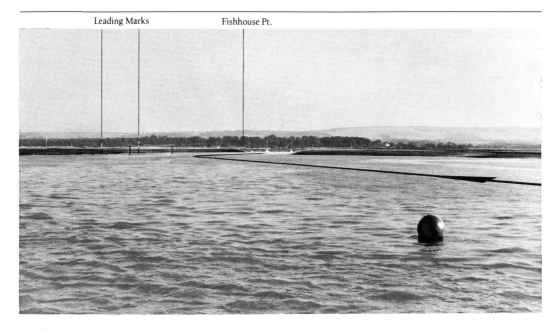

4.1. Newtown entrance from seaward. The leading marks are indicated and therefore the bar buoy should be left well to port.

will then be seen. The entrance lies between two shingle spits, at the east end of the shingle shore extending for ½ mile east of Hamstead Point, which is backed by a line of low trees for most of the distance. The leading marks consist of two beacon posts on the mud to the east of the entrance on the north side of Fishhouse Point. The outer one is painted with RW stripes and has a Y topmark and the inner bears a white disc within a black circle.

4.2. The leading marks at low water. Fishhouse Point is on the extreme right.

4.3. The river entrance with Fishhouse Point on the left. The yacht aground in the centre indicates the shingle bank which dries out. It is marked by green perches, sometimes weathered, but, as can be seen, these should be given a wide berth. This picture was taken at MLWS with an easterly wind and a low run of tide.

Bring these marks in line and stand in on their transit at approximately SE. The small spherical red bar buoy (but the bar is to the WSW of it) will be left nearly a cable to port. Continue on the transit leaving perches with red can topmarks to port and a small spherical green buoy to starboard, which marks the steep gravel bank on the west side. The outer leading beacon, which is near the edge of the channel, may be used as a port hand mark, then bear to starboard to leave to port Fishhouse Point and two port hand perches close to it.

The bed of the channel is uneven, with only about 3ft (0.9m) on the bar, increasing to 5ft (1.5m) and then to 7ft (2.1m) and 11ft (3.3m) before falling to 4ft (1.2m) SW of Fishhouse Pt. It then deepens to 9ft (2.7m) before decreasing gradually to 3ft (0.9m) off the junction with Causeway Lake. It is marked by several perches on the mud on each side, those with red can topmarks to port and those to starboard painted green, though they sometimes become weathered so that the colours may not immediately be recognized. Occasionally they get knocked down or their position altered.

Just inside the entrance two drying shingle banks lie on the starboard side of the channel. Despite their being marked by two or three green perches, strangers often run aground here by steering direct towards yachts at anchor or on moorings and leaving the perches on the wrong side. As will be seen from the chart, after the entrance has been passed, there is a pronounced bend in the river. It runs SE towards a red port hand perch with a can top, on the north side of the entrance of Clamerkin Lake, before bending round to the SSW, in the reach where a number of yachts on moorings lie in the centre of the channel. Note that on the south side of the entrance to Clamerkin Lake there is a green perch, which is a starboard mark when entering this channel but must be left to port when continuing up Newtown River. The channel is then easier to follow close to the yachts at moorings as the deep water (varies between 6ft and 4ft (1.8 and 1.2m)) is very narrow. Near the junction with Causeway Lake the depth falls to about 3ft (0.9m). Beyond this the water quickly shoals. At low tide there is little water in the upper tributaries, namely Western Haven and Shalfleet Lake: in fact, at low spring tides Shalfleet Lake dries out, although it is navigable at low water neap tides in a dinghy. The main arm of the harbour is only marked as far as the junction with Causeway Lake.

Clamerkin Lake is fairly deep, having over 4ft (1.2m) CD of water for a considerable distance. The channel is marked by occasional perches and one small G conical buoy (see photograph p. 39) but the line of yachts at anchor and moorings assists pilotage. There is danger from rifle practice at the top of the creek and in Spur Lake; red flags are flown during firing.

Lights: None in the river.

Moorings, Anchorage and Facilities
There is a good temporary anchorage during offshore winds outside the river near the position marked 1.2 metres on the chart, or further outside, finding a suitable depth by taking soundings. This is now much used, especially at neaps when there is more water at low tide, if

4.4. Looking up Newtown River. The yachts on moorings indicate the trend of the channel. The lower Hamstead landing is about two cables up on the starboard side.

N

RANGES

DANGER AREA
(Rifle Fire)

Power
Cable

·Bn   ·Bn   ·FS

·Bn   ·Bn

TO PORCHFIELD

NB

Scale in Cables
0   1   2   3   4   5

Scale in Kilometres
0   ½   1

Spur Lake

Saltings

Quay

Brick Works

Clamerkin Lake

Saltings

Path

NEWTOWN

Old Town Hall
(NT)

Newtown
Gravel Banks

03

06

27

09

03

Public Landing

Path

Path

N. Quay
& Shed

Paths

Causeway Lake

Corf Lake

Shalfleet Creek

Fishhouse
Pt.

W

RW

BAR   15

FG

Newtown River

1·2

S. Quay
Slip

Path

Shalfleet Mill

Shalfleet

82   R

0·3

1·2

Landing

Lower
Hamstead

Western Haven

Hamstead
Point

Path

3·6

Obsn

Dn

0·6

Hamstead

Fl(2)G 5s
G
HAMSTEAD
LEDGE

4.5. The small G buoy that now replaces one of the perches in Clamerkin Lake.

the river itself is crowded. The usual anchorage in the river is in about 9ft to 6ft (2.7m to 1.8m) in the first reach of the channel between the entrance and the permanent moorings belonging to local yachts - see below for possibility of hiring one. In strong northerly winds the entrance and anchorage can be rough near high water, especially on the first of the ebb at springs when the stream is strong. Better shelter is found farther up the river near the junction with Causeway Lake in about 3ft (0.9m) at CD plus 1½ft (0.5m) at MLWS or 4.8ft (1.5m) at MLWN, but the best positions are now occupied by permanent moorings. Centreboard or very light draft yachts, however, may be able to find snug anchorage beyond the permanent moorings and there is more water there at neap tides. There is also anchorage in 4ft (1.2m) CD (about 5½ or 6ft at ordinary springs) in the first reach of Clamerkin Lake which in some respects is the best.

Yachts are requested not to anchor beyond the anchorage limits marked by notice boards, owing to the proximity of oyster beds in Clamerkin Lake and Newtown River. Anchors should be buoyed when anchoring near permanent moorings especially in the main arm.

There are three visitor's moorings (conspicuous white buoys) in Clamerking Lake and there are three more white buoys in the main arm leading to Shalfleet. Application should be made to the Berthing Master (Mr. B. Smith. Tel. Calbourne 424). He or his Deputy may be found at the black shed by the quay. They visit yachts to collect harbour dues, which are payable for mooring or anchorage. They are well earned for without the River Committee there would, at times, be absolute chaos owing to too many yachts in too small an area. If they are not collected it is requested that any dues will be placed in the National Trust box behind the shed on the quay.

Newtown River: Soundings in metre. Add 0.5 m (1.6 ft) at MLWS, 1.5 m (4.8 ft) at MLWN. Based on British Admiralty Chart No. 2040, with the permission HM Stationery Office and of the Hydrographer of the Navy.

4.6. Shalfleet Quay.

There is a public landing on the east side of the river north of the quay. Facilities for yachts are limited, which is perhaps a good thing as the charm of the creeks lies in the lack of development of the unspoilt countryside. Limited repairs can be undertaken by Mr. Richard Seabroke, who can be contacted at the quay or at Marsh Farm (Tel. Calbourne 213) which can be reached by footpath from the quay. At Lower Hamstead on the west side of the river there is a private landing but yachtsmen are allowed to use it at their own risk. From the landing it is only 200 yards to the farm where there is a small licensed shop run by the farm. Alternatively, make a dinghy excursion to the quay by the old salting in Shalfleet Lake; then follow the track along to the bank of the creek to Shalfleet on a main bus route, where there is the New Inn and nearby, in Warlands Lane, a small shop and PO. There is a small yacht yard (Mr. Woodford) and slip at Shalfleet Quay and near high water the creek is navigable by shoal draft yachts thus far. Apply at the yacht yard for a mooring of which there are a fair number in the reach off the quay for craft of shoal draft.

The creeks provide interesting sailing for dinghy excursions and there are many splendid walks, of which perhaps the best is to Upper Hamstead along the shore or the wooded bank where there is a profusion of primroses and violets in the spring, but adders have also been seen there. The whole estuary and much of the surrounding land is the property of the National Trust and it is requested that the Trust's bye-laws be observed. The land and marshes near the creeks provide nesting places for countless sea and water birds. During the nesting season April-June inclusive 'No Landing' notices are placed on Fishhouse Point and it is hoped that yachtsmen will co-operate in the preservation of the birds which add so much interest to the surroundings.

5 Beaulieu River

Double High Water at entrance: Springs — 0h 45m Portsmouth and + 1h 20m; Neaps mean + 0h 5m.
Tidal Heights above datum at entrance approx: MHWS 12.2ft (3.7m) MLWS 1.9ft (0.6m) MHWN 10.2ft (3.1m) MLWN 5.2ft (1.6m).
Stream sets to the westward off East Lepe Buoy about — 1h 0m Portsmouth, and to the eastward about + 4h 45m Portsmouth.
Depths: Bar on leading line 2ft (0.6m) CD. The river bed is uneven with from a depth of 5ft (1.5m) up to 20ft (6.0m) as far as Buckler's Hard, except for a few shoaler patches referred to below.
Yacht Clubs: R Southampton YC, Beaulieu River SC.

OF ALL THE Solent creeks and harbours Beaulieu River is undoubtedly the most beautiful. From the entrance its wide channel leads west between marshes, the sanctuary of sea birds, and then takes a turn to the northward bringing the yachtsman within the 'perambulations of the Forest'.

Buckler's Hard, situated on the west bank about half way up the river was established by John, Duke of Montagu, in the eighteenth century and became the scene of shipbuilding activities. In the wide street between the cottages and Buckler's Hard lay piled the Forest oak from which the wooden walls of Nelson's days were built. The house of Henry Adams, the famous shipbuilder, is still standing, and is now preserved as 'The Master Builder's House' hotel.

From Buckler's Hard the river pursues a wandering course through the Forest for two miles, drying out at low water in the last reach leading to Beaulieu. Here there is the historic abbey, believed to have been founded by King John and built by the Cistercian monks in the year 1204. The monks were given a charter with the maximum possible privileges, which tradition attributes to the consequence of the King's bad dream after he had ordered his servants to trample certain monks under the feet of their horses. In more recent times the ancient rights of the monks, confirmed by various sovereigns to the successive owners of Beaulieu, were inherited by Lord Montagu and the Trustees of the Beaulieu Estate. These rights, almost without parallel in the British Isles, include ownership of the bed of the river and foreshore, flotsam, jetsam, lagan and wreck. From the yachtsmen's point of view the landowner's rights have been an advantage. They have prevented unsightly development and, besides keeping the river unspoilt, have led to the entrance and channel being properly boomed and the appointment of a Harbour Master who is most helpful to visiting yachtsmen, besides collecting the dues.

The Approach, Entrance and Channel

Approaching the entrance from the westward keep well off shore to avoid the shallow water off the Warren Flat and Beaulieu Spit until the conspicuous coastguard cottages, a white

boathouse and the conspciuous tripod dolphin (which bears a light Q R and a notice limiting speed to 5 knots) are identified and the entrance is opened up. The dolphin marks the west side of the entrance and stands in shallow water at the eastern end of Beaulieu Spit, which covers on the last quarter of the flood. The front leading mark has a white board with an angular top on the first port hand pile and the rear is a similar white mark on a pole. The latter is not so clear as it is among trees situated about 1½ cables west of the conspicuous ex-coastguard cottages and white boathouse on the shore. Bring the leading marks into line at 337° and stand in on their transit, which leaves the dolphin about ½ cable to port.

When approaching Beaulieu River from the eastward keep well clear of the shoals between Stansore Pt and Stone Pt, marked by three beacons (Q R) situated near the fathom (1.8m) line. See page 57 for information on cable area. Shoal water continues to extend about 3 cables from the shore west of the beacons, and it is simplest after passing the most westerly beacon to bring it into line with the middle beacon and sail on this stern transit until the leading marks for the river are brought into line, when proceed as before.

The transit of the leading marks at 337° leads on the extreme west side of the entrance channel so it is best to open the shore beacon slightly to the east. There is only about 2ft (0.6m) at CD (4ft MLWS) on the bar east of the tripod beacon, but the depth increases to 7ft (2.1m) and soon to over 20ft (6.0m) after the first leading mark is passed. The channel is clearly marked by piles with reflectors. On the port hand these are red piles (even numbers) with can tops and red reflectors and on the starboard hand green piles (odd numbers) with green conical tops and green reflectors. Booms and perches are placed on the edge of the mud and should not be approached closely.

As the shore is approached the entrance channel bends round to the west behind Beaulieu Spit into a long straight reach between mud banks on either side. The accompanying chart shows some of the depths in this first reach which carries a least depth of 7ft (2.1m) except for a 3ft (1.0m) shoal on the north side of the channel at the entrance of the Exbury Creek and another 2 cables beyond it.

The river begins to bend again off the jetty of the Beaulieu River SC at Need's Oar Point, turning to the NW and leading past Gin's Farm and the R Southampton YC. This reach is deep except in vicinity of a shoal on the east side shown on the chart. At Gin's Farm there is a hard and a private pier. A cable beyond this is the jetty and pontoon of the R Southampton YC, and the pile moorings reserved for the club. Here the river bends to NNE and then to N for the mile reach up to Gilbury Hard. The channel is wide and clear with a least depth of 5ft (1.5m) at CD but is 7ft (2.1m) and over for the most part. Off Gilbury Hard it turns sharply to the westward up to Buckler's Hard east of which there is a shoal stated to be rarely less than 4ft. Above Buckler's Hard the depths vary considerably from 3ft (0.9m) to 9ft (2.7m) as far as the pier at Spearbed Copse, and the channel is navigable with sufficient rise of tide as far as the brickworks at Bailey's Hard where there is a landing. Beyond this the river dries out

Beaulieu River: Soundings in metres. Add 0.5m (1.6ft) at MLWS, 1.5m (4.8ft) at MLWN. Based on British Admiralty Chart No. 2040, with the permission of HM Stationery Office and of the Hydrographer of the Navy.

5.1. Beaulieu River entrance looking north showing from the left the dolphin at the entrance with the *QR* light, the two leading marks, the back one partly hidden in the trees and the coastguard cottages on the right. The dolphin is left about ½ cable to port.

5.2. A nearer view of the leading marks.

at CD, though it can be used by light draft craft near high water up to Timbrell's Quay at Beaulieu. All the jetties on the river are private, but in addition to the hards mentioned there are landings at Gilbury Hard, a cable beyond the jetty, (Gilbury village and stores ¾ mile walk) and at Keeping Trees, ½ mile above Buckler's Hard.

Light: A light, Q R which must not be confused with the Q R lights on the three beacons off Stone Pt, is established on the outer tripod dolphin. This enables the river to be used at night with local knowledge, and given clear moonlight possibly also by strangers.

Bull Lake (or Bull Run): This swatchway has now been closed to navigation.

Moorings, Anchorage and Facilities

Beaulieu River is one of the few remaining places in the Solent where it is still possible for yachts to anchor. This is permitted in the first long reach between Lepe House and Need's Oar Pt, which provides over a mile of water sheltered by land on the north side and on the south by Beaulieu Spit, except for a swell at the eastern end at HW in strong southerly winds. Nearest landings are on the beach at the entrance, at the quay up Exbury creek, which dries at half tide, and at Need's Oar, where the club house of the Beaulieu River SC is nearby. The anchorage is far from facilities but the 2 miles up the river to Buckler's Hard do not take long with the aid of an outboard engine. A riding light is advisable as the channel is used at night. Anchorage outside is prohibited in the cable area as indicated on the chart.

5.3.   Starboard pile No. 15 and the entrance to Exbury   5.4.   Beaulieu River SC.
       Creek.

5.5.   Gin's Farm. R Southampton YC in the background.

5.6.   Buckler's Hard. The marina is about a cable beyond the jetty.

   The moorings in the river are all privately rented, but there are pile moorings to
accommodate about 100 visiting yachts. Application for a berth, or for the use of a mooring if
temporarily available should be make to the Harbour Master at Buckler's Hard (Mr W. H. J.
Grindey, Tel: Bucklers Hard 200/234). His office is at the Yacht Harbour. The Yacht Harbour
marina is only a cable above the Buckler's Hard jetty. Fuel and water can be had at the marina
fuelling jetty. All facilities are provided: Bucklers Hard Boat Builders Ltd (Tel: Bucklers Hard
214) for all yacht service, maintenance and chandlery: Bucklers Hard Garage and Marine for
servicing, overhauls and winterizing of inboard and outboard engines: Bucklers Hard Stores
(Tel: Bucklers Hard 293) is open seven days a week in season and will accept telephone orders
for collection including newspapers. Taxis can be ordered from Maurice Badlard Private Hire
(Tel: Beaulieu 612267).

5.7. Buckler's Hard Yacht Harbour. Fuel jetty on the left.

5.8. Buckler's Hard visitors' mooring piles.

In the small village, which consists of two widely spaced rows of cottages running down to the river, there is the Master Builder's House Hotel with restaurant and snack bar. The Maritime Museum (which is well worth seeing) is at the far end on the left, where there is the car park and Mulberry Tea Garden for light lunches and snacks. A footpath provides a pleasant walk along the river and through the woods to Beaulieu.

At Beaulieu landing can be made at high water. There is 5ft (1.5m) at Timbrell's Quay, where there is the Palace Quay boatyard, and light boats can be launched. The Abbey and Palace House and gardens and Motor Museum are open to visitors and there are a few shops, PO and an hotel.

6 Cowes and Medina River

High Water (Long): Springs mean — 0h 15m Portsmouth; Neaps mean + 0h 15m.
Tidal Heights: MHWS 13.9ft (4.2m), MLWS 1.9ft (0.6m), MHWN 11.4ft (3.3m), MLWN 5.6ft (1.7m).
Stream sets to the westward in Cowes Roads 1h 30m before local HW and to the eastward just before LW.
Depths: Except for a 5ft (1.5m) patch opposite East Cowes SC, there is a minimum of 8ft (2.4m) in the channel to within ½ mile of the Folly Inn, when depths fall to 3ft (0.9m) and then to 1ft (0.3m) off the light beacon, beyond which the channel soon dries out.
Yacht Clubs: Royal Yacht Squadron, Royal London Yacht Club, Royal Corinthian Yacht Club, Island Sailing Club, East Cowes Sailing Club, Cowes Corinthian Yacht Club, Gurnard Sailing Club.

THE DAYS OF the great schooners and cutters, with their famous owners and big professional crews, are long past and with them something of the splendour of Cowes has gone. Today the scene is basically amateur but infinitely broader and more active with the vast fleets of smaller yachts. Cowes Week, when coupled with the start of the Fastnet Race, provides the highlight which attracts yachtsmen the world over and creates what is probably the greatest and most vivid spectacle in international yacht racing.

Cowes is conveniently centred near the middle of the Island shore and at no time in its history has the town been more dedicated to yachting and providing amenities for visiting yachtsmen.

Approach and Entrance

Approach from the west is easy by following the line of the coast from Egypt Point about a cable offshore or less according to the state of the tide and draft of the yacht. As racing men know, sometimes to their cost, there are rocky edges extending in places almost ½ cable seawards. The streams are strong. When approaching from the west, or leaving the harbour bound west, an early eddy running contrary to the main flood stream will be found inshore between the Squadron and Egypt Point.

From the eastward keep well to seaward to avoid the Shrape Mud and shallow water north and NW of it. At night a look out should be kept for unlit buoys.

The fairway lies on the west side of the harbour and is marked by buoys. On the east side there is a long breakwater which serves to scour the tide and to provide protection from winds from this quarter. On this side the water is shallow but at ordinary springs there is 2ft (0.6m) and at neaps 5½ft (1.7m) more than is shown on the chart. The area is occupied by large numbers of private moorings and if sailing among them care should be taken to avoid being set by the stream on to moored yachts.

Parts of the fairway may be busy with racing craft on big regatta days which, by courtesy, should be given right-of-way, especially as seconds count when they are working into position

6.1. The Royal Yacht Squadron Castle and Cowes foreshore towards Egypt Point.

for the start of a race or approaching the finishing line. Red Funnel ferries and ships add to the congestion despite the care and consideration with which they are handled, but the channel is easy to follow past the Island Sailing Club, the Red Funnel pontoon, the marina and visitors' moorings. The channel narrows where the floating bridge chain ferry crosses it - and note that the chains lie at least 2ft (0.6m) above the bottom in mid-channel. Near the floating bridge and for a good ¼ mile beyond it the wind is often flukey owing to high ground and proximity of buildings. Beyond the chain ferry there are no navigation buoys but the deep water lies in the area between the pile mooring trots and heavy moorings. Except for the patch shown on the chart opposite the East Cowes SC, the minimum depth is 8ft (2.4m) to within ½ mile (1km) of the Folly Inn. *See River Medina.*

The maximum speed permitted for all vessels within Cowes Harbour is 6 knots over the ground, but speed should be reduced in the vicinity of yachts on moorings or as seamanship requires. Water skiing or planing is prohibited.

Lights: The Prince Consort buoy, situated about ½ mile NE of the entrance exhibits a *V Q* light and port hand No 4 buoy is *Fl R 5s.* The light on the end of the breakwater is *Q R.* The leading lights in transit at 164° consist of a white light (*Iso 2s 6M*) on the post at the seaward

Cowes: Soundings in metres. Add 0.6m (1.9ft) at MLWS, 1.7m (5.6ft) at MLWN. Based on British Admiralty Chart No. 2793, with the permission of HM Stationery Office and of the Hydrographer of the Navy.

end of Watch House landing and a rear light (*Iso R 2s 3M*) on the Dolphin on the south side of Fountain Pier. There are fixed red (to port) and green (to starboard) lights on the various wharfs and pontoons and up the river there is a *V Q (3) 5s* light on Medham beacon and a *Q G* light on the beacon south of the Folly Inn.

Moorings and Anchorages

There are four large temporary visitors' moorings situated off the Parade, on the starboard hand just past the Royal Yacht Squadron, convenient for Customs clearance. The Ancasta Marina lies on the starboard hand just beyond the Fountain Pier and the Red Funnel Pontoon in the area previously occupied by mooring piles. This marina welcomes and provides for visiting yachtsmen, even those staying only overnight. Yachts berth alongside floating pontoons close to the centre of the town and facilities, but two pile berths where yachts moor abreast of each other remain available just south of the marina.

The swinging moorings on the east side of the harbour are private, or specially laid for racing classes during regattas, and must not be picked up by visitors, though it is sometimes possible to obtain the temporary use of one on application to the Harbour Master, Capt H. N. J. Wrigley, (Tel: IoW 293952.)

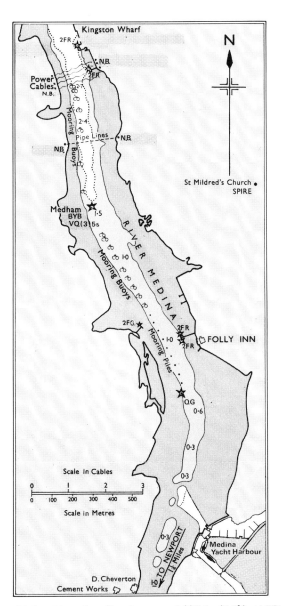

Medina River: Soundings in metres. Add 0.7m (2.5ft) at MLWS. 1.7m (5.7ft) at M.WN. Based on British Admiralty Chart No. 2793, with the permission of HM Stationery Office and of the Hydrographer of the Navy.

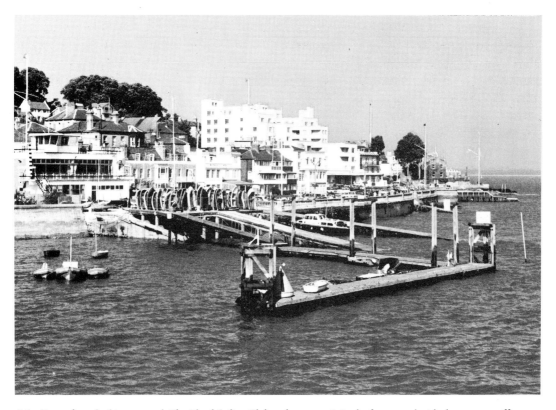

6.2. Cowes front looking seaward. The Island Sailing Club and pontoon is in the foreground with the customs office just beyond it. The prominent white building is Osborne Court flats and the Royal Yacht Squadron is on the extreme right.

As the harbour is exposed to all northerly winds it can be very uncomfortable in strong winds and gales from this quarter, when it may be better to move up the river. Visitors' moorings (clearly marked by notice boards) will be found there on both sides of the river on piles in the reach to the south of the floating bridge to suit any size of yacht. The Cowes Marina, built by Wilment Marine, has visitors' berths at East Cowes some three cables above the chain ferry ('floating bridge') on the east bank of the river. There are also pile moorings for small visiting yachts in the Folly reach, opposite the Folly Inn. Beyond them is the Medina Yacht Harbour - see River Medina.

Anchorage is to seaward of existing mooring buoys which lie to the east of No 4 R buoy. Cowes Roads are exposed and the streams through them are strong so the anchorage is used mostly by larger yachts. Smaller craft usually anchor in shallower water, with the help of soundings, closer in to the north and NW of the end of the breakwater where there is plenty of water at neaps. In settled weather and offshore winds, anchorage is possible, but not recommended, off the Parade to the west of the Squadron, a position which is not far from the town though subject to the swell from passing ships.

Anchors should be buoyed anywhere in the vicinity of Cowes in case of fouling mooring chains, particularly those of big commercial buoys which often stretch a long distance. In fact, the chains of the Trinity House mooring buoy, for example, extend 500ft east and west, though in the harbour the scope is much shorter. Anchorage is prohibited (1) in the fairway (2) in the mooring area on the east side of the harbour (3) where there are cables or obstructions indicated by notice boards such as just beyond the floating bridge or off Kingston Power station (4) in the Folly Reach.

Facilities
There are many public landings among which the following may be mentioned in order of approach: several on the Parade, Watch House Slip (nearest to Customs) two farther south leading to High Street, south side Fountain pontoon and other landings south of it. Whitegates pontoon is the most convenient beyond the Floating bridge and just beyond it is the National Sailing Centre pontoon. Landing is also possible by permission at various yacht yards. At East Cowes there are three slipways but at present no convenient hards or pontoons.

As stated before, Cowes is dedicated to yachting and provides exceptionally good facilities of all kinds within easy distance of the harbour. There are no less than seven yacht clubs, including the Royal Yacht Squadron which remains the premier yacht club and the Island Sailing Club, which is very go-ahead and has excellent facilities with a pontoon in the season for members and visiting yachtsmen introduced by members. It is hospitable towards foreign yachtsmen, especially to visitors in Cowes Week.

Yacht building and repairs are undertaken at Lallow's, Souter's, Ancasta and several other yards. Fuel and water are available at Lallow's jetty and other yacht yards. There are also fresh

6.3. The Ancasta Marina.

water points at Watch House slipway, Whitegates pontoon and Old Town Quay. Among the well known names in the yachting industry are Ratsey & Lapthorn Sailmakers, Beken's (photographs), Pascall Atkeys (chandlers) and Benzie (yachting jewellery). In addition there are engineers and riggers and pretty well any yachting requirement is available. EC Wednesday. Customs at Watch House slip. The best known hotel is the Fountain, but there are several others and numerous pubs and boarding houses. Cowes is a convenient harbour in which to leave a yacht under surveillance during an owner's absence by arrangement with the Harbour Master.

There is a good bus service connecting with all parts of the Island. Red Funnel steamers and hydrofoil service to Southampton.

RIVER MEDINA

The river cuts a long groove through to the centre of the Island from Cowes to Newport, the capital. It is in part commercial, but the land in the background on either side is high and to the east it is well wooded so the scene is by no means unattractive. The channel is not buoyed but it lies between mooring piles or mooring buoys and it is not difficult to follow with depths of 8ft (2.4m) to Kingston Power Station and ¼ mile beyond, when it becomes shallower and soon falls to 3ft (0.9m) as the Folly reach is entered. The river is spanned by submarine power cables and a pipe line, the positions being marked by notice boards to indicate prohibited anchorage.

From Kingston to the Folly Inn the channel is best followed by leaving the line of moorings and Medham Beacon close to starboard. On an ordinary spring tide yachts of 5ft (1.5m) draft can sail up to the Folly Point and there is plenty of water at neaps, though larger yachts should bring up to the piles in 6ft (1.8m) to 8ft (2.4m) about ½ mile to the northward.

Off the Folly Inn there are pile moorings suitable at ordinary springs for yachts drawing 4½ft (1.4m) or, say, 7ft to 8ft (1.8m to 2.4m) at neaps, but anchorage is not permitted. There is a landing pontoon at the jetty and a scrubbing hard which can be used by arrangement at the inn, where there is a buffet bar and meals can be had to order. Fresh water is laid to the pontoon and there is a small shop. Calor gas is available. In all, it is a quiet and pleasant place to bring up, and there is a path along the river bank the whole way to Newport.

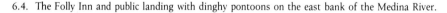

6.4. The Folly Inn and public landing with dinghy pontoons on the east bank of the Medina River.

6.5   The entrance to the Medina Yacht Harbour on the east bank above the Folly Inn.

The Medina Yacht Harbour (ex Medway Queen Marina) lies about 4 cables South of the Folly Inn with berths for 240 yachts in the locked basin. The approach channel marked by port hand piles and starboard buoys is dredged to 3ft (0.9m) MLWS. The depth in the basin is maintained at about 8ft (2.4m). The lock is operated on request 3 hours either side of high water when 8ft (2.4m) of water will be found. It is not normally lit but can be floodlit if a yacht is expected at night. Manager: Paul Merritt. (Tel: IoW 526733).

Above the Folly the depths soon begin to decrease but the river is navigable with sufficient rise of tide by ships to Newport. The upper reaches provide interesting sailing. There are pontoons for bilge-keel craft at Newport (EC Thursday).

6.6.   The visitor's pontoon and Newport.

7 Southampton Water

Double High Water: Springs — 0h 30m and + 1h 30m Portsmouth; Neaps mean + 0h 15m. At Springs after about 3 hours flood there is a stand for 1½ hours, followed by a 3½ hours rise. The ebb runs strongly for 3½ hours attaining maximum rate 2 hours after second HW.
Tidal Heights: Southampton, above datum. MHWS 15ft (4.6m) MLWS 1.5ft (0.5m) MHWN 11.3ft (3.9m) MLWN 5.8ft (1.9m).
Depths: Ample at any state of the tide.
Yacht Clubs: R Southampton YC, Southampton SC, Ashlett SC, Eling SC, Hythe SC, Marchwood YC, Netley Cliff SC, Weston SC.

WITH ITS DEEP and easy approach and double high water, Southampton has been a natural port and centre of shipbuilding from time immemorial. Inevitably too, it has been an objective of raids from the sea by Danes and the French. Nevertheless, it was the Norman Conquest which brought greatly increased trade to Southampton. The Bargate was built and the prosperous part of the town lay between this and the present Royal Pier, where some of it is still to be seen. The Middle Ages brought increased prosperity especially in the wool and wine trades. It was not until the middle of the eighteenth century that the port began its modern development and from then onwards grew rapidly in stature.

In particular, the name of Southampton has been linked with those of the great transatlantic liners. It was the home port of many famous ships, among which were the ill-fated *Titanic*, the *Mauretania* and *Lusitania* and the Queens, *Mary*, *Elizabeth* and *Elizabeth II*, besides their competitors among the great ships of the world seeking the honour of the Blue Riband. Passenger liners feature less in the news today, but Southampton remains a port for many of the leading cruise lines. The importance of the port is increased by the huge oil refinery at Fawley and the petroleum terminal on the opposite side of Southampton Water.

Southampton Water provides a considerable length for day cruising with the added interest of its shipping. The port itself and the city are the administrative centre of the whole area, with Customs, Lloyds Surveyors and the Ministry of Transport for the registration of yachts as well as of ships. The town offers every kind of yachting facility.

The Approach and Channel

Southampton Water and its approaches are wide and deep, and very well marked, so that the only point in navigation lies in keeping clear of the shipping in the fairways. The Southampton Dock Board southern boundary line runs from Stansore Point to Hill Head and there is a port bye-law which reads: 'Sailing vessels must not make use of the deep water channel in such a way as to cause obstruction to the large steam vessels using the Port.' Another bye-law prohibits yachts entering the area bounded by Bourne Gap Buoy, Calshot Spit Light Float, Castle

7.1. Calshot Spit Light Float.

Point Buoy, Reach Buoy, Calshot Buoy and North Thorn Buoy. Anchorage in the fairway including the Test and Itchen is also forbidden. The bye-laws should be strictly observed, as apart from the law, it is only common sense to keep out of the way of vessels, particularly tankers, which are very difficult to manoeuvre in the narrow water available for their deep draft, and which are virtually impossible to stop quickly.

So far as yacht racing is concerned the problem has to some extent been relieved by the laying of special buoys, which provide turning-marks clear of the deep channels. The problem should be a lesser one when cruising, as there is plenty of room in the approaches to Southampton to navigate either outside the deep fairways or on the edge of them without obstructing the big ships, crossing the fairways only when the channel is clear. What is important is to anticipate the movements of the big ships. Leaving Southampton Water and rounding usually close east of Calshot Light Float, they proceed down the Western Approach Channel. Thence they continue either in deep water west to the Needles (Signal W over Answering pennant) or they round the West Bramble buoy, turning to pass between the South Bramble and Prince Consort Buoy and east to Spithead. (Signal E over Answering pennant). Smaller ships may proceed east via the North Channel. When a ship is not under command or unable to avoid an approaching vessel 'she shall sound one long blast followed by two short blasts so that the approaching vessel can take action to avoid collision'.

Approaching from the west a good offing should be given to the shoals off Stone and Stansore Points, leaving to port three beacons, Q R, situated near the 1 fathom (1.8m) line. Do not steer direct from the westerly beacon to the next at LW as the shoal bulges about 50 yards seaward between them. Power cables (from 33,000 to 132,000 volts), telephone cables and gas pipes cross the Solent from shore to shore on this prohibited anchorage, which extends approximately from Lepe to Gurnard Head on the west side and between Stansore Point and Egypt Point on the east. Damage can be caused even by a small yacht attempting to winch up an anchor fouled on a cable or by impact or grounding on a cable in shallow water such as lies northward of the three beacons. The owner of a yacht causing damage to a cable may render himself liable for loss and repair costs running into a very large sum.

The Western Approach for big ships lies between the flats off the Hampshire coast and the

7.2. Calshot Castle and
Black Jack

Bramble Bank. On the NW side it is marked by NE Gurnard buoy (*Fl (3) R 10s*) and Bourne Gap buoy (*Fl R 3s*) and Calshot Spit light-float (*Fl 5s Horn (2)*). There is plenty of water for most yachts west of the buoys as shown on the chart, but Calshot Spit dries out in a SE direction for ½ mile from the beach and most Solent yachts leave the light-float about a cable and Castle Point buoy (*I Q R 10s*) ½ cable to starboard, which gives 5ft at MLWS. Greater liberties can be taken with sufficient rise of tide. The next red port hand buoy is Black Jack (*Fl (2) R 4s*) but this is near the NE edge of Calshot Spit so it should either be passed on the correct side or left very close to starboard. Beyond this buoy the water deepens and course may be laid to leave Calshot Castle jetty to port or to cross over to the east side of Southampton Water either to proceed to Hamble or up to Southampton.

On the SE side the Western Approach is marked by the West Bramble (*V Q (9) 10s*), Thorn Knoll (*Fl G 5s*), North Thorn (*Q G*) and Calshot (*V Q*) buoys. On this side also, yachts can avoid the fairway by going on the wrong side of these buoys, and leaving to starboard the yellow Spanker and the green W Knoll and E Knoll buoys. The Bramble Bank varies from time to time in position and depth and is composed of shingle. There is an orange Radar beacon about 1 cable SE of the worst part, which at present dries about 5ft (1.5m) at CD. There is also the East Knoll shoal but this has 1ft (0.3m) over it at CD, and lies to the SW of Hill Head buoy. To clear the Brambles on the west side, if bound from Cowes to Southampton, keep west of the line of the Royal Yacht Squadron, the West Knoll green buoy and the light-float, and vice versa.

At night it is simplest to keep in or near to Western Approach channel as it is clearly marked by the light buoys shown on the chart. During fog pilotage is assisted by the bell, *15 sec*, on W Bramble, the Horn (2) on Calshot light-float and the bell, *30 sec* on Calshot N Car Buoy.

From the east the approach is equally easy. The channel lies between the land with its offlying shoals on the starboard hand and the buoys on the east side of the Brambles: E Bramble (*V Q (3) 5s*), Hill Head (*Fl R 2.5s*). Yachts can pass nearly ¼ mile eastward of the

Southampton Water: Soundings in metres, add 0.6m (1.9ft) at MLWS, 1.7m (5.6ft) at MLWN. Based on surveys with the permission of British Transport Docks Board, Southampton. Approaches based on Chart No. 1905, with the permission of HMS Stationery Office and of the Hydrographer of the Navy.

Calshot buoy (V Q) and *Bell 30s*, in 15ft (4.6m) and shallow draft craft will find nearly 1½ fathoms (2.7m) nearly a mile to the eastward, but must stand away from the shore when Calshot Spit Lightfloat bears west as the mud flats on the east side extend a long way off the land. The Coronation Y conical buoy (*Fl Y 5s*) is starboard hand but may be left a cable to port. The small G conical Bald Head starboard hand buoy is moored close to the drying shoal extending off the shore.

The Main Channel

Southampton Water main shipping channel is marked on the port hand (west side) by red can buoys exhibiting *red occulting* or *red flashing lights*: there are also lights at either end of Fawley jetty (*2FR vert*). The starboard (east side) is marked by conical green buys showing green flashing lights. In addition, there are occasional R (port) and G (starboard) buoys nearer the edge of the mud for the use of ships of less draft. The channel itself is clear and wide and the general direction up to the Dockhead is about NW Mag.

On the west side of Southampton Water, after passing Calshot Castle the Esso Refinery jetties are the first conspicuous features, and extend a long way from the shore, on which large oil reservoirs will be seen. At night the whole area is illuminated by the lights and the glare of the excess gas flare stacks reflected in the clouds. For the next 2 miles beyond the refineries the west shore possesses no particular features except for the measured distance beacons with white triangles situated high on the mud flats. Three red buoys are passed and westward of the third is the Admiralty jetty (*2 FG*), for the old Coastal Forces Base off which there are many large mooring buoys. The Hythe Sailing Club is on the shore just south of it. Hythe ferry pier is ½ mile beyond the Admiralty jetty and once past this the deep channel lies on the east side near the docks.

The starboard hand (east) of Southampton Water is equally clearly marked. Once inside Calshot, after passing the Reach buoy, (*Fl (3) G 10s*), the first buoy on the starboard hand is the Hook (*Q G* and *bell*) but this lies on the edge of the big ship fairway, and from a yachtsman's point of view may almost be considered as placed in mid-channel. Half a mile east of the Hook is the Coronation buoy, previously mentioned. Hamble Point S Car YB buoy (*Q (6) + L Fl 15s*) is 1 mile farther up, which marks the port side of the entrance to Hamble River, but is a starboard buoy when proceeding up Southampton Water. On Hamble Point will be seen the Cougar Marine works, and about a mile farther up will be seen a number of oil storage tanks and the Shell Jetty. To the north of this is Hawker Siddeley Aviation Ltd, off which there are transit beacons which govern the controlled anchorage for ships of over 300ft. Hamble Spit which dries out at CD, projects into Southampton Water approximately to a line from Hamble Point Buoy to the end of the Shell Jetty and should be left well to starboard, although in summer months it is marked by the yellow Cathead racing buoy.

Following up the line of the coast for another 2 miles, the site of the Royal Victoria Hospital at Netley, of which only the central dome remains, is brought abeam. Above Netley the mud runs out a greater distance from the shore and Western Shelf dries out at CD; at low water even a yacht of light draught will have to keep near to the buoyed channel.

7.3. Hook buoy (*QG and Bell*).

At the Dockhead, which is conspicuous in the middle of Southampton Water, the channel divides, the River Test continuing in a NW direction and the River Itchen branching away to the NNE. Both rivers are referred to under separate headings.

Fawley Basin. The entrance to the 12ft (3.6m) dredged channel, leading to the Fawley Power Station, lies ¼ mile beyond Calshot Castle on the west side of Southampton Water. It is very clearly marked by pile beacons, with occasional lights at night when in use by ships. There are moorings for local yachts, belonging to members of the Fawley Power Station Social and Sports Club, on the south side between No 10 beacon and the entrance channel and water intake of the Power Station. Across this entrance there is a floating oil boom, the apex of which is secured by anchors with buoys, which are sometimes mistaken by strangers for mooring buoys. Yachts must keep clear of the boom, as there is an undercurrent into the channel. It may be possible on application to obtain the use of a vacant mooring or to anchor close to the port hand beacons temporarily but the slope of the mud is very steep. Visiting yachts must on no account obstruct ships using the dredged channel to the power station, and

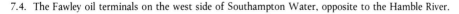

7.4. The Fawley oil terminals on the west side of Southampton Water, opposite to the Hamble River.

61

enquiry should be made about their movements. The public landing on the south side of the entrance channel has been reinstated.

Ashlett Creek. The entrance to this creek is just over ½ mile above Fawley Basin and is close to the Fawley R buoy which lies a cable south of the southern end of the Esso jetties. The creek appears to be ½ cable wide at high water but most of it is very shallow, drying up to 8ft (2.4m) near Ashlett, except for a very narrow channel which is little more than a gutter winding through the mud. Nevertheless, it provides interesting water for centre-board and light draft craft. The active Esso Sailing Club has a club house near the head of the creek; it is the authority that maintains the navigation and (seasonal) racing marks in the creek.

Keel yachts can use the channel with sufficient rise of tide, but 4ft (1.2m) draft is about the maximum without local knowledge, as the channel is difficult to follow at HW springs when the marshes are covered. At low water, keel yachts must sit in mud or dry out alongside the quay.

When entering, leave Fawley buoy (which is in shallow water) close to port and come on to a course of approx 254°. The leading marks that used to give this transit are much decayed, difficult to find and are not being replaced. Ahead should be seen the first of three small R can buoys. At times there is also a spherical Y racing mark (seasonal and not shown on the chartlet) marked ASHLETT, moored on the starboard side of the channel. Follow the three R port hand buoys round the first 90° bend into the SE reach, then round the G starboard hand buoy at the second 90° bend into a long reach to the SW. The channel is very narrow at this bend and one should keep close to the buoy. This next leg of the channel is nearly straight; leading marks are the electricity pole (*RW hor*) near the Sailing Club and the chimney of the red brick cottage with slate roof behind the quay. There are some posts and withies remaining and some with top-marks (G triangles to starboard: R squares to port) but these are placed well up on the mud.

The third 90° bend is to NW, the channel being close to the stern moorings of the boats at the SW bank. Keep well clear of the speed limit Notice Board as there is a short gravel spit running SW of it. Pass close to the post with R square top-mark, which is just north of the end of the public landing stage steps. The channel curves slightly in a thin 'S' bend to a sharp hairpin bend round a post with R square top-mark which leave close to port. After rounding this, head straight back towards the Club flagstaff, then follow the line of moorings to starboard, leaving the SLIP buoy (R) to port. Visiting yachts should now head for the public quay at the head of creek, with moorings to starboard and mud berths to port.

There is also a South Channel, along the line of the Outfall marked by Y beacons, south of the main creek, but this should not be attempted without local knowledge.

Note that old mooring chains cross the creek in a SE direction to the starboard buoy at the first bend near the entrance and east to west at the second bend.

Ashlett is pretty and consists of a quay and hard, a few houses, the old mill and The Jolly Sailor's inn. Yachts can berth at the quay which dries 7ft (2.1m) CD, and which is suitable for a scrub. Launching site at hard. Water at the Inn, stores at Fawley, ½ mile distant.

7.5. Netley Great Dome with the Netley Cliff SC below.

7.6. Ashlett Mill (now an Esso club) and the quay at high water.

7.7. The Esso SC at Ashlett.

63

7.8 The electricity pole (RW hor), near the ESSO SC, that acts as one of the leading marks to Ashlett Creek.

Hythe Marina Village

This development is (1987) in course of construction on the reclaimed land just north west of Hythe. The marina is in use and a number of houses are in occupation. The entrance is marked by piles, the outer pair comprising an east cardinal mark (*Q (3) 10s*) and a port hand mark (*Fl R (2) 5s*). The channel, dredged to 2m, leads to lock gates open three hours either side of high water. Visitors are welcome and when completed there will be every facility available. Radio watch is kept on Channel M. A public hard is included in the development.

7.9 The entrance to the channel leading to Hythe Marina (1986).

Moorings and Anchorages

Anchorage is possible in Southampton water anywhere clear of the ship fairways and moorings and outside the prohibited areas. Anchorage should be sought under a weather shore, according to the wind, and it is wise to buoy the anchor to avoid foul mooring chains or foul bottom. Swell is caused by passing ships. The following are the places most commonly used:

1. *Hamble River*. See Chapter 8.

2. *Off Royal Pier*. There are Docks Board moorings for large yachts.

3. *Netley*. Half a mile north of Netley Dome, there is a good hard with the Netley Abbey Boat Yard adjacent to it. Stores at Netley ¼ mile and bus service. Moorings for small local yachts. The anchorage lies outside these on a lee shore in westerly winds.

4. *Hythe*. Between the line of Hythe Pier and the Admiralty Jetty there is only from 1 to 3ft (0.3 to 0.9m) CD. Farther out from the shore there is 5 to 6ft (1.5 to 1.8m). The anchorage is reasonable in westerly winds but take care to anchor clear of moorings. Landing is at Hythe pierhead, from which ferries run to Southampton and an electric train to the shore. Marine Services Ltd yacht yard is at the inner end of the pier and has moorings and a service launch. The Hythe Sailing Club is at the shore end of the Admiralty Jetty, to the south of which the Club has many small moorings. In Hythe itself there is an hotel, shops and facilities of a small town. EC Wednesday.

5. *Rivers Test and Itchen*. See below.

Facilities

Southampton is the administrative centre for the Solent, and has the Weather Centre, (Tel: Southampton 228844). Recorded weather forecasts for the coastal area between Poole Harbour and Chichester can be called on Southampton 8091. There are good facilities for yachts. F. Smith & Son are official agents for charts of which they keep a wide stock, besides nautical instruments and books. They are also compass adjusters. Tillings supply yacht chandlery, as do the yacht yards. Water at Town Quay, Royal Pier or yacht yards. Shops of all kinds. Many of the large shops close all day Mondays, but most of them have early closing on Wednesday. Several hotels and restaurants. Excellent railway services, buses to all parts of Hampshire and motor coaches to London and elsewhere. Red Funnel steamer and hydrofoil service to Cowes. A marina is planned at the Town Quay. Ocean Village Marina has already (1986) been opened at the Princess Alexandra Dock, see River Itchen.

RIVERS TEST AND ITCHEN

The River Test. Leaving the Dockhead to starboard and proceeding up the River Test in a NW direction, the Queen Elizabeth II Terminal and the Ocean Dock will be passed. The deep channel lies on the docks side of the river, whereas beyond the port hand red buoys there is the Gymp shoal and foul ground.

Continuing up the river the Town Quay and Royal Pier will lie to starboard and half-a-mile

7.10. The southerly point of Southampton Docks. River Test to port. River Itchen to starboard.

7.11. The southernmost of the leading beacons for the Marchwood channel.

7.12. The more northerly leading beacon for the Marchwood channel. It is often obscured by moored yachts.

farther up, the river is divided into two parts, leaving a narrow shoal between the two. The northern is the deep dredged channel running past the Western Docks, at the end of which is the King George V graving dock and the container berths. The southern side is the Marchwood Channel, and leads up past Cracknore Hard, Husband's jetty and SW to Marchwood Basin.

To follow the southern part of the river, alter course off the Royal Pier and steer towards No 2 Swinging Ground buoy (red can). Just short of this the yacht will come on to the leading marks for the dredged Marchwood Channel. These are two beacons, the first with a triangle topmark and the second with a diamond topmark. Keeping these in transit at 297°, a Y can buoy (marking the NE corner of the basin dredged to Marchwood Power Station quay) will be left to port and a beacon with a square topmark to starboard. The latter stands in the middle of the shoal between the Marchwood Channel and the northern channel along the docks.

The dredged area of the Marchwood Channel, which leads only to the entrance of Marchwood Basin, ends about ½ cable east of the first beacon with triangle top. Here treat the two beacons as starboard hand marks, passing close to them sailing through the area of the Marchwood SC moorings where the shallowest lie in 1ft (0.3m) CD. Well to starboard will be left No 4 and No 6 red Swinging Ground buoys, which are on the north side of the middle ground.

After passing the second beacon bear to port, leaving to port No 8 Swinging Ground buoy (red), to enter the dredged channel for the new container berths.

Alternatively, instead of following the Marchwood Channel, the northern deep ship channel can be used, finally shaping a course leaving No 8 Swinging Ground buoy to port and entering the dredged channel and swinging ground.

Then follow up the river channel, marked by beacons, until arriving at a S Car YB beacon topped by two cones which marks the junction of two channels.

The northern arm, which is the Test River, leads to Redbridge wharfs. It is marked by appropriate beacons, but it dries out and is of little interest except for centreboard sailing. The western arm leads to Eling where shoal draft yachts can dry out on the mud. Leave the junction beacon and also the five beacons with triangle topmarks to starboard. The channel is extremely narrow and dries 2ft (0.6m) at CD close to banks which dry 7ft (2.1m). Just short of Eling, after passing under power cables, it turns sharply to the SW into the basin where the best water is on the starboard side. In the middle of the basin is a mud bank, between the shallow gutters of water on the north and south sides. Strangers may find the north side easier, passing the big quay and bringing up at or before the small quay, alongside which there is about 6ft (1.8m) at HW springs. Local advice is needed if wishing to remain at low water as the basin is crowded by light draft yachts and small craft. Shops in the built-up area on the north side. EC Wednesday. Launching site at hard on north side. Eling Sailing Club has a landing pontoon, winter quarters and scrubbing hard for its members. The Anchor Inn overlooks the basin.

The R Corps of Transport Depot and the R Engineer YC have moorings for their member's yachts downstream of Husband's Shipyard and Marchwood YC has the mooring in the area south of the transit beacons for the Marchwood Channel. The latter has its club house and a slip at the hard beyond Marchwood Power Station. Enquiries about the possibility of temporary vacant moorings may be made at Husband's shipyard or the club. The shipyard is principally commercial, but also undertakes yacht repairs, especially of large yachts. The yard supplies fuel and water and has a ferry launch to Southampton Town Quay. The Ship Inn at Cracknore Hard is adjacent but no other facilities are close at hand.

The River Itchen. This river now accommodates three marinas and has become much used by yachts.

The entrance lies on the east side of the Dockhead between the docks and the mud flats on the starboard hand marked by Weston Shelf conical green buoy (*Fl (3) G 15s*), No 1 Swinging Ground green buoy (*Oc G 4s*) and two dolphins No 1 (*Q G*) and No 2 (*Fl G 5s*) and the Weston jetty (*2 FG vert*), beyond which is No 3 dolphin (*Fl G 7s*) and No 4 (*Q G*), while to port there is the Bank beacon (*QR*) and the entrance to Ocean Village Marina.

About a mile from the entrance, the Itchen bridge (24.4m) crosses the river. The river then

7.13. The entrance to Ocean Village Marina.

7.14. Shamrock Quay Marina.

bears NW - and is marked on the port hand by Crosshouse beacon (*Oc R 5s*) and a little farther up by Chapel beacon (*Fl G 3s*) on the starboard hand.

The channel starts a bend to the north east, the deep water being on the west side. About five cables on, the Shamrock Quay Marina is located on the port hand in the old Camper & Nicholson premises. There is then a semi-circular bend right round to the west which is marked by beacons. Pontoons will be left to starboard before arriving off Kemp's Quay Marina which is also left to starboard. Beyond this the river leads east for 3 cables to Northam Bridge and the channel lies on the south side with a very wide expanse of mud on the north. Beyond the road bridge the Itchen is only 2 or 3ft (0.6 to 0.9m) deep and not marked, but there are two yards: the Rampart Boatyard and the Belsize Boatyard.

Ocean Village Marina is under construction (1987) in what was Princes Alexandra Dock. Traffic through the marina entrance is controlled by light signals: 3FG = "GO": 3FR = "STOP": 3 Fl R = "ALL STOP": 2 FG over 1 FW = "TWO WAY TRAFFIC'. A watch is kept on Channel M.

Shamrock Quay is well established and has all facilities less fuel. There are nearby chandlery, bars and restaurant in a busy and attractive development.

Kemp's Quay Marina is now enlarged to 200 berths. It can provide diesel fuel, showers, toilets, water and electricity. This claims to be one of the least expensive marinas in the Solent area.

8 Hamble River & Titchfield Haven

Double High Water: Springs — 0h 25m and + 1h 35m Portsmouth; Neaps mean + 0h 20m. At springs after about 3 hours flood there is a stand for 1½ hours, followed by a 3½ hours rise. The ebb runs strongly for 3½ hours attaining maximum rate 2 hours after second HW.

Tidal Heights above datum at Calshot Castle: MHWS 14.5ft (4.4m) MLWS 2.1ft (0.6m) MHWN 12ft (3.6m) MLWN 6ft (1.8m)

Stream sets in the Solent west about — 1h 0m Portsmouth and east shortly after + 4h 0m. Note an early stream sets SE at about + 3h 0m. Portsmouth on the east side of the entrance to Southampton Water opposite Calshot LV when the main Solent stream is still running west.

Depths above datum: For the average yacht of 6ft (1.8m) draft the Hamble River is deep, but in reality the bottom is very uneven, much of it being 2 fathoms (3.6m) and more, with shoal patches such as in the vicinity of the Spit Pile 5ft (1.5m) at CD and only 8ft (2.4m) off the School of Navigation pier. For this reason it is best to take the depth as 7ft (2.1m) which gives about 9ft (2.7m) at MLWS up to Badman Creek. Above this there is something in the nature of a bar with only 5ft (1.5m), after which the depths are 6 to 7ft (1.8 to 2.1m) up to Bursledon Bridge.

Yacht Clubs: R Southern YC, R Thames YC, R Air Force YC, Household Division YC, Hamble River SC, Warsash SC.

FOR A CONSIDERABLE time the Hamble River has been one of the largest concentrated yachting centres in the British Isles. Developments continue at what can only be described as a fantastic rate, and the river is packed with yachts the whole 2½ miles from Cougar Marine near the entrance up to Bursledon Bridge. In addition to rows of pile moorings, there are four large well managed and well equipped marinas. What is so interesting is the extraordinary variety of yachts in the river. There are many famous ocean racers and new yachts of every kind to the latest designs, both sail and power, besides great numbers of first rate cruising yachts. Smaller standard types can be counted by the hundred and the picture is broadened by old-timers and other yachts of individual character.

Historically, the river, in common with other Solent harbours, has been the scene of many attacks by invaders from the sea. Cedric and Cynric are said to have landed in the year 519 - the year in which the final defeat of the Britons took place. It is certain that it was much attacked in later years by the Danes. Swanwick is one of the place names in Hampshire which are probably of Danish origin - perhaps originally Sweinwyk.

The river is now controlled by a more orthodox body, the Hampshire County Council, who charge relatively lower dues than were extracted by the Danes. They are actively continuing the developments in the river started by the former Southampton Harbour Board and British Transport Dock Board, Southampton. The former bye-laws still apply. Motor yachts and yachts under auxiliary power must keep to starboard side of the fairway and navigate with care and at a speed such as will not cause damage or danger. Speeds should certainly be low, otherwise the wash causes the utmost inconvenience to those aboard the hundreds of yachts on moorings and can be a danger to children in boats.

8.1. Hamble Point south cardinal buoy.

The Approach and Channel

The sailing directions for Southampton Water will bring a yacht inside Calshot Castle, when course should be shaped for the Hook green pillar buoy (Q G), which lies in the centre of Southampton Water about ¼ mile NE of Calshot Castle. From this point Hamble Point Buoy is situated N by W only ¾ mile distant. When approaching from the east, the Hook will be left to the westward, and the course will set to leave the Coronation Buoy (Fl Y 5s) to starboard, or not more than a cable to port as it is not far off the shoal on the east side of Southampton Water. The unlit Baldhead Buoy (G) must be left to starboard.

When Hamble Point S Car buoy (Q (6) + L Fl 15s) is brought abeam a series of piles marking the channel will be seen. These make the channel clear, but if a transit is desired it will be a red diamond day mark on Pile No 6 beacon on the port side of the channel in line 345° with a red triangle day mark on a white pole beacon on Hamble common. The port hand piles are fluorescent red with can tops and are marked with even numbers 2, 4, 6, 8 and 10. Do not bring these port hand marks too close aboard. The starboard hand piles are green with green triangular topmarks. They bear odd numbers from 1 to 9, and also should not be approached closely.

The channel bends towards the NE at No 6 pile and the inner entrance to the river is between the Cougar Marine works on the port hand and the end of the Warsash Jetty on the

8.2. The inner entrance of the river with Cougar Marine on the port side. The Harbour Master's office at Warsash can just be seen on the right of the picture.

8.3. The rather startling end of the Warsash Jetty.

starboard hand. Here the fairway is on the starboard side of the river. Once inside the river there are fewer navigation marks, but the channel is fairly obvious as there are numbers of yachts moored on both sides of the fairway.

The village of Warsash lies to starboard, where will be seen the prominent black and white Harbour Master's office building and his pier. Opposite Warsash there is the Hamble Point Marina. A ferry service, dating from some 500 years, still operates between Warsash and Hamble. Hamble itself is about ½ mile farther up the river on the port hand. The Southern YC, RAFYC and Port Hamble Marina will be seen.

The bends in the river are shown on the chart. As the first bend to the NNW is approached about ¼ mile above the Port Hamble Marina there was an isolated gravel bank. Many yachts used to run aground on this but it is now west of the port hand piles. On the port hand, just before Badnam Creek, yachtsmen will find the Mercury Yacht Harbour, and beyond it lies the extensive Lincegrove Marsh, which is broken up into many small shallow creeks, and is marked by a white beacon. On the opposite side of the river is a beacon and tide gauge marking the edge of the extensive mud flats on the starboard hand. The river then takes a NE direction to Swanwick and the fairway lies between mooring piles on either hand.

At the end of this reach is a sharp turn from NE to NW and a stranger approaching the bend will see yachts apparently lying to piles in the middle of the river and more yachts not far from them lying on moorings on the east side. This is because there is a mud shoal at the bend on the port side extending almost halfway across the river, which is marked by a red beacon. This must be left to port as also the line of mooring piles beyond it but the yachts on moorings are left to starboard.

8.4. Warsash and the Harbour Master's modern office building and his pier in the foreground.

8.5. The fuelling berth at Hamble Point Marina.

8.6. The sharp bend at Swanwick shore leading to Moody's yard and Swanwick Marina.

Above Swanwick there are two short reaches; first, north-west to Bursledon leaving Moody's pier and large marina to starboard and then north-east up to the bridge. The deep channel is much narrower in these upper reaches and lies close to the piles on the port hand. The wind is fickle when it is blowing off the high ground on the west side. There is a shoal on the starboard side of the channel close above Moody's Swanwick Marina.

Beyond Bursledon Bridge there is a railway bridge and a motorway bridge. In the reach between them there are houseboats and motor yachts lying on moorings. At high water the channel is navigable in a dinghy or by light draft craft as far as Botley, about 3 miles above the bridge; in fact, the channel is fairly wide and over a fathom deep for much of the distance. The river runs between densely wooded shores and is very pretty.

Lights: Leading lights are established which lead up the outer two reaches of the river channel as far as Warsash. The first pair consist of the light *(Oc (2) R 12s)* on No 6 Pile beacon in line at 345° with a rear beacon *(QR)* on Hamble Common, which has an arc of 8°. The lights for the next transit up to Warsash are a light *(Q G)* on the Warsash Shore Beacon and a light *(Iso G 6s)* over an arc of 8° on the rear beacon, the transit being 026°. This will lead to a position abreast the Warsash Jetty *(2 FR vert)*. Beyond this, the river is marked as far as Bursledon Point beacon by four lights *(Fl R 2s)* on piles on the port hand and by four lights *(Fl G 2s)* on the starboard hand, as well as many fixed lights R and G, as appropriate, marking the various jetties and pontoons.

Hamble River: Soundings in metres. Add 0.6 m (2.1 ft) at MLWS, 1.8 m (6.0 ft) at MLWN. Based on surveys with the permission of British Transport Docks Board, Southampton and Hampshire County Council.

75

Moorings, Anchorage and Facilities

There is no room left in the Hamble River for anchoring, except in between No 6 port hand pile and No 9 Starboard pile, clear of the landing transit. Here it is rough in fresh SW winds and during daytime it is disturbed by the wakes of constantly passing motor yachts, so it is useful only if arriving at night waiting for daylight to continue up the river.

The Harbour Master (Capt C. J. Nicholl OBE) and his Assistant (Mr K. V. G. Willis) have an office and jetty at Warsash shore (Tel: Locks Heath 6387). The Administrative Officer (Mr E. J. Sainsbury) mans the office during office hours. Application should be made to the Harbour Master for berthing, but the following positions are available for visiting yachts and bear notices to this effect.

Warsash. Piles on the port hand of the main fairway Nos B1 to 4.

Hamble. Opposite Port Hamble piles on the starboard side Nos 9 to 16.

There are three public scrubbing hards. The Warsash Hard just off The Rising Sun Hotel; the Mercury Scrubbing Hard, where one is advised to berth N of the pile; and the Lands End Hard opposite Swanwick Marina. All three are operated on a first-come-first-served basis and free of charge for the first 48 hours.

Berths may also be available on application at Port Hamble and Swanwick marinas, as also at the Mercury Yacht Harbour and Hamble Point Marina. It is wise to book in advance. The yacht yards may also be able to advise on moorings temporarily available in the absence of their owners, and the yacht clubs have moorings which if temporarily vacant may be available, on application, to members of affiliated clubs or other approved visitors.

Water and fuel may be had at any of the yacht marinas or yacht yards. Customs' launches for clearance. The Customs' office is at Port Hamble (Tel: Southampton 45200) and arrangements may be made there for bonded stores from Southampton.

At Warsash there is the Sea Fever Yacht chandlery and nearby is The Rising Sun Hotel and the Solent School of Yachting. There is a car park and hard suitable for launching. Restaurants include Eduardo's Cortigo, Great Harry (carvery), Chon Chola (tandoori), New Lucky House (English/Chinese) and the Village Pantry (open for breakfast). In the village there are a PO, banks and several small shops. EC Thursday. Buses to Gosport, Burlesdon and Southampton.

At Hamble there is the large Port Hamble Marina operated by Rank Marine International Ltd with the usual marina facilities, including fuel. J. R. Williams (Chandlery) Ltd at Hamble make and repair sails. Launching sites at the public hard or Port Hamble. There are other chandlers, yacht agents, three banks and shops of most kinds in the village. EC Wednesday. Restaurants: Bugle Inn, Beths, Bon Appetit and King & Queen. Buses to Woolston, Bursledon and Southampton. The R Southern YC is close to the hard. South of this is a car park (and another is in the village) and the dinghy enclosure. The RAFYC just south of Port Hamble Ltd at the end of the Ropewalk, and Hamble River SC by the ferry hard.

Farther up the river at Badnam Creek on the west side ¾ mile (1.2km) from Hamble is the Mercury Yacht Harbour, also operated by Rank Marine International. There are the usual marina arrangements for water and electricity, but for repairs, laying-up, other yard work and for fuel, yachts are taken to Port Hamble. In the next reach there is the jetty (with fuel and water) of Universal Shipyards (Solent) Ltd. At Swanwick Shore, farther up the river where it bends to NW is a public hard (launching site), the jetty and dinghy landing pontoon of A. H. Moody and Son Ltd.

At this old established family yard with a new look, there is every conceivable requirement, including yacht agency and chandlers, for yachts of all sizes. The large Swanwick Marina adjoins the yard and has been considerably extended on the NW end. On the opposite side of the main road is Greenham Marine (electronics) and a garage. Bruce Banks Sails at Sarisbury and Ian Proctor Metal Masts are in easy reach by car or bus. There is a grocer near Moody's and 100 yards up the Swanwick road is another grocer, PO and butcher. Hot and cold snacks at The Spinnaker, restaurant at the Old Ship (best to book in advance) or across the bridge at The Swan. Buses to Southampton, Fareham, Gosport and Warsash.

The village of Bursledon is a little higher up the river on the west side with landing at the steps by the Jolly Sailor or at the hard by the bridge, but the end of the latter dries out before LW. The Elephant Boat Yard for yachts up to about 10 tons TM is just beyond the Jolly Sailor and near the bridge is the larger Trapper Yachts Ltd with alongside moorings. Foulkes & Son's boatyard is just beyond the railway bridge. Launching site (often congested) at Land's End a cable SE of Jolly Sailor, at the bridge hard or by arrangement with Trapper's or at the boatyards above the bridges. Grocers and PO at Old Bursledon. Restaurant at Swan Hotel and up the hill at the Crow's Nest. Station at Bursledon, main road bus stop at Swan and the Hamble bus stop at Crow's Nest. Beyond the motorway bridge, on the west side, is the Upper Hamble Country Park.

8.7. The popular *JOLLY SAILOR* opposite the Swanwick Marina.

TITCHFIELD HAVEN

Titchfield Haven lies 3 miles SE of Hamble River and at the west end of Hill Head. This attractive Lilliputian harbour consists of a mud camber at the entrance of the River Meon south of the sluice under the coast road. It is protected from north and west but is very small and dries out at low water springs, so that it is only suitable for centre-board dinghies and very shoal draft yachts, such as twin keelers which can take the bottom. Anchorage outside is possible in offshore winds but it will be far from the haven, as the sand and shingle dries out ¼ mile at LW springs, so that even entering it by dinghy involves a wait for sufficient rise of tide (allowing for drying 5 to 7ft (1.5 to 2.1m) at CD, except when sufficient river water is coming down.

The Camber lies behind a shingle spit to the west of which is the coastal road above the sea wall, parking space and further west many bathing huts. To the northward of the spit there is

8.8. The shallow channel which is formed by the outflow from the River Meon on the right bends almost parallel with the shore and is marked by two perches on the starboard hand. This picture near low water shows where it enters. The Camber.

a large, white house, a clump of trees just east of it and a large red brick house with other houses still further eastwards. The best approach (which can be made only with sufficient rise of tide over the drying sand and shingle) is with the brick house bearing 020°. This leads about 100 yards ESE of the end of the spit. A small beacon with diamond topmark (one of the marks for the Hill Head Sailing Club's start line) is in the channel and should be left close to starboard before altering course in a curve to the west almost parallel with the land.

The Hill Head Sailing Club occupies a prominent position on the sea wall just to the east of the entrance. The Club (Tel: Stubbington 664843) should be consulted if wishing to remain and dry out as most of the camber is occupied by private moorings. A visiting yacht could well bring to temporarily near the bridge, but the bottom is foul and old timbers and piles make it a bad spot to dry out. At Hill Head, ½ mile east of the haven, on the bus route, is the Osborne View Hotel (Tel: Stubbington 662018), garage, shops, PO and the Hill Head Chandlers (Tel: Stubbington 664621).

8.9. Titchfield Haven can only be approached with sufficient rise of tide over the drying sand and shingle. The modern building on the sea wall is the Hill Head SC. Opposite can be seen a small metal beacon, which is in the middle of what channel there is.

9 Wootton Creek

High Water: *Springs mean - 0h 10m Portsmouth; Neaps +* 0h 5m.
Tidal Heights above datum: MHWS 14.9ft (4.5m) MLWS 2.3ft (0.7m) MHWN 12.2ft (3.6m) MLWN 6ft (1.7m).
Stream sets outside to the westward about — 1h 30m Portsmouth and to the eastward + 4h 20m.
Depths: Dredged up to 6ft (1.8m) CD as far as the ferry terminal but silting occurs. Shallow beyond.
Yacht Club: Royal Victoria Yacht Club.

WOOTTON IS ONE of the Solent creeks with charm and individuality but unfortunately of recent years there has been considerable silting in the pool which provides the only part where a visiting yacht can remain at low water, unless she is of shoal draft and can lie up the river on the mud. Nevertheless, when there is room the pool can still be used at neap tides by yachts up to 4½ft (1.4m) draft or a little more - see below.

Quarr Abbey is situated ½ mile to the eastward. Very little of the old abbey itself remains beyond the ruins of the Abbot's kitchen and fragments of the wall. This was originally built in the reign of Henry I, but the present building was erected less than 100 years ago by Benedictine monks. It is said to be one of the largest buildings built of bricks, and was designed by one of the monks.

9.1. Wootton Beacon.

9.2. The leading mark triangles on the west shore, if proceeding up the creek. They are not so easily seen now that there is a small wooden building behind them.

The Approach, Entrance and Creek

The entrance to Wootton Creek lies two miles west of Ryde Pier and is clearly marked by Wootton Beacon (Q) and three further beacons on the west side of the channel. No special directions are necessary for the approach from the east, but, as the mud flats run out a long way, the shore must be given a wide berth. Sail from the outer end of Ryde Pier towards Barton Point, which is the point beyond King's Quay, 1½ miles east of Old Castle Point. Then, when Wootton Beacon is seen steer in towards it.

To approach from the west, an imaginary line from Old Castle Point to the shore end of Ryde Pier will clear all dangers handsomely, and as soon as Wootton Bridge village opens up, Wootton rocks will have been passed.

Having arrived off the beacons, alter course to steer up the straight channel leaving the four beacons close to starboard as the fairway, which is dredged to 6ft (1.8m) CD, is very narrow and the flats on its east side are unmarked. There is little room for tacking and the car ferries require most of the fairway, especially at low water, when it is best to wait until the channel is clear of any ferry seen approaching. Although the channel is deep up to the ferry pier, there is no point in entering it until there is sufficient rise of tide to sail up the river or to enter the pool, which now dries at MLWS.

If continuing to the pool, then on arrival at No 3 Beacon head for the end of the Ferry Pier and leave this 6ft to port. Once past the end of the pier the yacht will be in the pool where yachts lie at the visitors' piles and visitors' moorings.

If wishing to proceed up Wootton Creek instead of to the pool, there is a turn to starboard after passing No 3 Beacon. The channel is marked by R (port hand) and G (starboard hand) buoys and by leading marks which can be seen on the shore below the woods to the west. These consist of two white triangles on frames (see photograph).

The best indication of the channel after the leading marks is to follow the line of moored craft leaving them to starboard. The channel is narrow but with a sufficient rise of tide a 3½ft (1.1m) draft yacht can get right up to the top of the creek.

Lights: The beacons carry lights: Wootton Beacon [Q], No 1 [Fl G 3s], No. 2 [Fl (2) G 5s], No 3 [Q G].

Moorings, Anchorage and Facilities

Wootton Creek comes under the authority of the Queen's Harbour Master at Portsmouth. His authority over the allocation of moorings and navigation in the creek is exercised through a private association, the Wootton Creek Fairways Committee (Hon Sec Mr R. W. Perraton, The Moorings, Sloop Lane, Wootton Bridge). Advice on moorings can best be obtained from the Manageress of the Royal Victoria Yacht Club, Miss Sheila Cronin (Tel: IoW 882325). Yachts must not at any time anchor in the fairway or where the car ferries turn to the hard. The ferries use the channel by day and night. There is no water in the pool at MLWS and it dries out at CD, but the mud is soft and yachts of moderate draft and twin keel craft can take the ground and remain upright.

Except in strong northerly or easterly winds, the pool is a good place in which to bring up. There are both mooring buoys and mooring piles for visitors. The Royal Victoria Yacht Club welcomes visiting yachtsmen. The club has a dinghy hard, car park, changing-rooms and bar. Water, stores, bread, milk etc, can be obtained there and also meals. Nearby at Fishbourne there is a garage, and the Fishbourne Inn, which serves meals. There is a launching site at HW.

In the upper reaches of the creek, the narrow channel is also occupied by moorings, but anchorage is possible on the mud for shoal draft craft, such as twin keelers, which can dry out. At the top of the creek there is a public landing on the west side. This will give access to some small boatyards. On the east side of the creek close to the bridge there are marine engineers. At Wootton Village there are garage, butchers, grocers, PO, bakers. EC Thursday. Good bus service on main road to Ryde and Newport.

9.3. The Royal Victoria Yacht Club and slipway.

Anchorage Outside: Temporary anchorage is possible outside in moderate offshore winds, preferably to west of Wootton Bn, and there is a popular anchorage at week-ends further to the west in Osborne Bay. A good position is off the HM Hard, ½ mile west of Barton Point, but this is within the grounds of Osborne House and landing is not permitted. The anchorage (taking soundings to find the right depth) is reasonably sheltered from W and S winds and the stream is weak.

KING'S QUAY CREEK

This shallow trickle of water lies about a mile NW of Wootton, and looks from the sea to be larger than it is in reality. There is no neighbouring village, and the creek is equally difficult to approach either from land or sea, but, nevertheless, is attractive.

Years ago small yachts occasionally entered King's Quay and anchored among the exceptionally beautiful surroundings, but the channel is now unmarked. The creek itself is very narrow and winds between steep mud banks, but is worth exploring on a rising tide in a shallow draft craft or a centreboard dinghy.

At low water there is but a trickle in the 'Gutter', as it used to be called. The entrance is difficult to recognise from the north and is to the west of the little marshy valley which the gutter drains. A careful approach to the shore-line on a south westerly course should be made on a rising tide. There is now (1986) little to indicate the best course of approach and a preliminary recce by dinghy is recommended. At high water the marshes are mostly covered, the banks of the gutter will not be seen and entry without prior knowledge very difficult. The

9.4. The visitors' pile mooring at high water.   9.5. The visitors' buoys at low water.

gutter winds through the marshes towards the woods, where it takes a sharp turn to the north west coming finally to a pool just below a decayed stone bridge and barrage. In this pool some 4 feet of water remains when the gutter has virtually dried out.

The banks are private property and the bottom of the creek is rented from the Crown by the Nature Conservancy which administers and wardens some 40 acres of the area as a nature reserve. Landing is forbidden and the landing of dogs, in particular, would be very unwelcome.

Wootton Creek: Soundings in metres. Add 0.7m (4.5ft) at MLWS, 1.8m (6.0ft) at MLWN. Based on British Admiralty Chart No. 394, with the permission of HM Stationery Office and of the Hydrographer of the Navy.

10 Portsmouth Harbour

Tidal Heights above datum: MHWS 15.4ft (4.7m) MLWS 2ft (0.6m) MHWN 12.5ft (3.8m) MLWN 5.8ft (1.7m). Flood 7 hours. Ebb 5 hours.
Stream sets to the NW outside at Spithead about — 2h 0m Portsmouth and to the SE about + 3h 30m Portsmouth, but the direction of the streams vary in the approach in relation to the local Portsmouth streams.
Depths: Ample at any state of the tide in the main ship channel.
Principal Yacht Clubs: R Albert YC, Royal Naval SA (and Service clubs), Hardway SC, Portsmouth SC, Gosport Cruising Club, Portsmouth Harbour Cruising Club.

PORTSMOUTH HAS BEEN closely linked with the Navy from the Middle Ages down to the Napoleonic wars and to present times. Nelson's *Victory* is open to visitors in the oldest dry dock in the world, and the frigate *Foudroyant*, built only 12 years after Trafalgar, is moored in the harbour and is reputed to be the oldest ship afloat. Although guided missile ships now replace the frigates of old, Portsmouth Harbour remains predominantly associated with the Royal Navy and comes under the jurisdiction of the Queen's Harbour Master.

The harbour covers an area of some 15 square miles which, apart from the dock area, consists of mud flats intersected by deeper creeks, of which Fareham and Portchester are the principal - *see next chapter*. Increasing use of the harbour has been made by yachtsmen in recent years, with Camper and Nicholson's marina near the entrance and club or private yacht moorings in almost every accessible part where permission has been given to lay them. There is plenty of local racing, and at Southsea the Royal Albert YC provides the starting line for the majority of ocean races and JOG events.

The Approach and Entrance

Straightforward chart work is all that is required for entry to Portsmouth, as the fairway is deep enough for an aircraft carrier and is well marked. Except at LW springs there is also enough water for most yachts on each side of the buoyed channel clear of the big ship fairway.

Approaching from the west it is usually quickest to follow the swashway used by the Portsmouth-Ryde ferries, which leads between the Hamilton Bank on its NW side and the Spit Bank on the SE side. The transit for this swashway has traditionally been the conspicuous white Naval Memorial on the Southsea shore, about ¼ mile east of Clarence Pier, in line with St Jude's Church at 047° but this will shortly change, since a planned block of flats will obstruct the view of St. Jude's Church. Except at LW springs it is not necessary to adhere exactly to the transit. When No. 2 red can buoy is abeam, alter course to port up the fairway to the boat channel - see p. 86.

Alternatively, with sufficient rise of tide and moderate weather, the inner swashway (not to be used by vessels 20m and over in length), affords a short cut westward of Hamilton Bank in

War Memorial   St Jude's Church

10.1. Leading marks for swashway between Spit and Hamilton Banks. St. Jude's church spire in line with the war memorial at 047° (Subject to change). Royal Albert YC signal station to left of the memorial.

Round Tower   Tank

10.2 The leading marks for the inner swashway are the western edge of the conspicuous tank in line with the western extremity of the round tower at 029°.

1ft (0.3m) least water. The transit is the west side of a high conspicuous tank in line with the west extremity of Round Tower at 029°. However, there is only a difference of about 2ft (0.6m) in being on or off the correct transit. Local yachtsmen often merely follow the Haslar shore, keeping about a cable off it, with sufficient rise of tide, but this is not recommended in strong S to E winds, owing to the cross seas washing back from the sea wall.

From the eastward, vessels proceed off the Horse Sand Fort, up the buoyed channel towards Southsea Castle lighthouse in line with St Jude's Church spire at 003° and then alter course at Castle conical G buoy to follow the fairway to the entrance. If coming from Langstone or Chichester Harbours, distance can be saved by taking the gap in the submerged barrier ¾ mile south of Southsea Beach. *See Chapter 13.*

Approaches to Portsmouth Harbour: Soundings in metres. Add 0.6 m (2.0 ft) at MLWS, 1.7 m (5.8 ft) at MLWN. Based on British Admiralty Chart No. 394, with the permission of HM Stationery Office and of the Hydrographer of the Navy.

87

Boat Channel

There is a boat channel exclusively for vessels under 20m long on the west side of the entrance. Such vessels must enter the harbour through the Boat channel or close inshore on the east side of the entrance, but must leave only through the boat channel. Vessels with engines must use them between No 4 buoy and Ballast Buoy.

10.3. No. 4 Bar buoy, with its injunction 'Small craft use engine. Use small boat channel'.

10.5. Ballast Buoy. The northern end of the small boat channel.

The flood tide starts at + 5h 30m Portsmouth and runs easy for 3 hours, and then strong for 4 hours; the ebb starts at + 15m Portsmouth and runs easy for one hour increasing to maximum on the 3rd and 4th hour, attaining 5 knots at springs, and then eases. At the entrance of the harbour, however, owing to the mass of water running out of the creeks, the ebb continues to run hard for longer, and only slackens during the last ¾ hour. Yachtsmen are not advised to attempt entry at the 3rd and 4th hours of the ebb at springs, particularly when strong SE winds against a fast ebb will cause big seas just outside the entrance. When sailing against the stream it should be remembered that there is slacker water on either shore and sometimes a helpful eddy on the east side as far as Round Tower. Caution must be taken to keep out of the way of HM ships, RFA tankers etc, when entering - see signals below:

1. **Day.** Red flag with white diagonal bar.
    Night. Red light over two green lights vertical. No vessel is to leave or enter the Harbour Channel, or approach from seaward N of Outer Spit buoy.
2. **Day.** Red flag with white diagonal bar over one black ball. No vessel is to enter the Harbour Channel from seaward. Outgoing vessels may proceed.
3. **Day.** One black ball over red flag with white diagonal bar. No vessel may leave the harbour, but ingoing vessels may enter.

4. **Day.** Large black pennant.
    Night. White light over two red vertical. No vessel is to anchor in the Man-of-War anchorage at Spithead.
5. **Day.** International Code Pendant superior to Pendant zero. HM ship entering, leaving or shifting berth. Keep clear.
6. **Day.** International Code Pendant superior to Pendant nine.
    Night. Three green lights vertical. Warning HM ship under way. All vessels give a wide berth.
7. **Day.** International Code Pendant superior to flags NE.
    Night. Green over red light. Proceed with great caution at easy speed. (Signal from Blockhouse Signal Station when ships - other than car ferries - leave the Camber.)
8. **Day.** Flag E.
    Night. Red light, amber light. Submarine entering or leaving Haslar Lake. Light flashes when submarine under way. Keep clear.
9. **Day.** International Code Pendant superior to Flag A.
    Night. Two red lights horizontal. Night, by diving boat all round red light in stern and bows. Have divers down.

Local Sound Signals: *These are not Fog Signals* (seldom used)

Signal	Meaning
–	Am steaming ahead.
– –	Am stopped. Sounded: Power driven vessels in risk of collision.
. . . . .	Am about to turn round to starboard.
. . . . . .	Am about to turn round to port. Sounded: Power driven vessels including a tug with tow.
. . . .	Am unable to keep out of your way. All vessels keep clear.

Should the above signals be observed after the yacht is in the channel, then she should leave or keep to the side of the fairway until the Naval vessel has passed, which can usually be done by yachts with perfect safety. In particular, yachts must keep absolutely clear of large Naval vessels in the narrow harbour entrance between Fort Blockhouse and the Round Tower and of course should be using the boat channel.

Lights: At night an incoming vessel should keep in the white sector of Southsea Castle light, *Iso 2s Dir WRG*, entering the ship fairway between the Outer Spit S Cardinal buoy *Q (6) + L Fl 15s* and the starboard hand Horse Sand buoy *Fl G 2.5s*. Thence proceed by chart in the well-marked channel. Fort Blockhouse at the entrance to the harbour has a *Dir WRG light* and incoming vessels should keep in the White sector.

Moorings, Anchorage and Facilities

As stated earlier, the Queen's Harbour Master is vested with jurisdiction within Portsmouth Harbour and, indeed, outside from the Needles to the Nab. His office is within the Naval Dockyard, so it is best to contact him by telephone, (Portsmouth 822351, ext. 3344), as moorings (other than those allotted to clubs, yacht yards and licence holders) are under his control, which also extends to anchorages.

A visiting yachtsman will have to obtain the use of a mooring or marina berth at least temporarily. If possible a booking should be made in advance, as few anchorages are available owing to prohibited areas, fairways for shipping and cables. The bottom is foul in many parts, so anchors should always have a trip line. The following yacht bases are listed in order of approach:

1. Main Gate
2. Public Telephones
3. Marina Office
4. Laundrette
5. Toilets/Showers
6. Marina Club
7. Yacht Stores
8. Fuel Barge
9. Repairs Office
10. Lucas Upperdeck Chandlery
11. Marina Diving Centre
12. Ancasta Brokerage
13. Sail Repair Depository
14. Scrub Off Berth
    (book at Marina office)
15. Short Term Car Park
16. Tourist Information Office
17. Gosport — Portsmouth Ferry
18. Town Centre
19. Waste Oil Depository
20. Waste Containers
21. Weather Forecast
22. Taxis

10.4. Camper & Nicholson Marina layout.

10.6. View over Camper & Nicholson Marina to Portsmouth. HMS Victory's masts in the background.

(a) **Anchorage Outside.** The Royal Albert Yacht Club, (Tel: Portsmouth 825924) has a dinghy slipway and a few moorings off Southsea Beach near the War Memorial and it may be possible to use one if permission is obtained from the club. There is room to anchor, clear of the moorings, but the position is uncomfortable except in offshore winds; there is a swell from passing vessels and it is far from facilities.

(b) **The Camber.** This is the commercial harbour of Portsmouth, situated just within the entrance on the east side. The Camber is used by the Isle of Wight car ferries and is usually packed with coasters, lighters and fishing boats, so it is not suitable for visiting yachts.

(c) **Haslar Lake.** This creek lies on the west side just round Fort Blockhouse. The channel is deep and lies along the SW side between the jetty (where submarines berth) and an extensive mud flat on the NW side, marked by dolphins. It then turns west to Haslar bridge and the depth decreases to 6ft (1.8m) CD. Yachts with lowering masts can pass under the bridge into the continuation of the creek which is called Alverstoke Lake. The channel is marked by piles but is very shallow.

The Joint Services Sail Training Centre operates from a complex of pontoons at the south west of Haslar Lake, near Haslar bridge, and there are many Service owned craft moored there. There are also pontoons and moorings on the north-west side. There is no specific provision for visiting yachts. Anchorage is limited and the bottom is foul. All facilities at Gosport.

(d) **Gosport.** Camper & Nicholson's marina is situated a cable above the ferry landing stage at Gosport, and has extensive facilities for yachts of all sizes. (Tel: Gosport 542811). Water laid on at pontoons. Fuel at jetty. Chandlery and all yard services. VHF watch is kept on Channel M - Callsign: 'CAMPER BASE'.

Beyond Camper & Nicholson's marina lies the Gosport Borough Yacht Harbour in the Cold Harbour. Both marinas are largely enclosed by a long, open-piled oil fuel jetty used by naval tankers. The Gosport Borough Yacht Harbour contains sets of double moorings, let on a long-term basis, but visitors are accommodated if there are temporary vacancies. Application should be made at the blue hut on the quay. Vessels may also make fast alongside the Town Quay, but this dries out and is never very pleasant. The adjacent scrubbing piles on the hard may be used on application. A Gosport marina is planned for the area of the mud bank west of Ballast buoy.

Besides the facilities already mentioned, there are shops of all kinds in the town including yacht chandlers (EC Wednesday, Gosport and Portsmouth; Thursday, Southsea) and also small restaurants and many pubs. Ferries to Portsmouth and buses to all parts. Landing steps (drying) near the ferry, and public launching site at Gosport Borough Yacht Harbour.

(e) **Weevil Lake and Forton Lake.** All available space in Weevil Lake is occupied by permanent moorings. The entrance lies north of the Cold Harbour immediately beyond the long jetty. This is left to port and a mud bank marked by piles lies on the starboard hand. The channel then turns sharply northward passing behind Burrow Island before bending to the west, where a wooden foot bridge separates it from Forton Lake. Depths in Weevil Lake are from 20ft (6.1m) at the entrance decreasing to 6ft (1.8m). It dries out at CD near the foot bridge (which can be opened by appointment by Admiralty police in gate house) and Forton Lake also dries out.

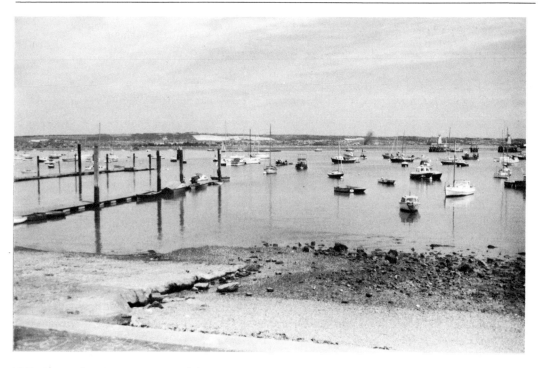

10.7.   The Hardway SC pontoons. Two of the Reserve Dolphins can be seen in the right background.

(f) **Hardway**. See Chart on page 94. This centre lies on the west side of the harbour about ¼ mile beyond the Sultan landing stage owned by the Admiralty, above the junction of Fareham and Portchester Lakes. Here the Hardway Sailing Club, (Tel: Gosport 581875), is very active and hospitable. Every available space is now occupied by moorings off the club and to the north and south of it, on both sides of the channel. There is even an overflow of moorings for small cruising yachts in the entrance of Portchester and Bombketch Lakes. The mooring area near the club is protected from westerly winds and there is a public hard and pontoons. The sailing club maintains a visitors' trot of 5 fore and aft moorings off their pontoons, which has water laid on. There are so many other moorings that there is always the possibility of one being temporarily vacant, for which enquiry should be made at the club house. The club has a scrubbing grid, 6ft (1.8m) and launching site adjacent. Marine shop and fuels nearby. Other shops and pubs up the road facing the Hardway and a restaurant near Vosper's jetty. Short walk to bus stop for Gosport and Fareham.

(g) **Fareham and Portchester** - see next chapter.

Communications. Express trains from Portsmouth Harbour Station and Town Station. British Railway Ferries to Ryde, IoW, adjacent Harbour Station. Car ferries to Wootton, IoW, from Camber. Buses from Portsmouth and Gosport ferry landings.

11 Fareham and Portchester Lakes

High Water: About + 0h 20m Portsmouth.
Tidal Heights: Fareham above datum: MHWS 13.2ft (4.0m) MLWS 1.8ft (0.5m) MHWN 10.5ft (3.2m) MLWN 5.0ft (1.5m).
Local streams: Shortly after HW the ebb runs for about 4¾ hours, followed by 3 hours slack before 4 hours flood.
Yacht Clubs: Fareham Sailing and Motor Boat Club, Portchester SC, Portsmouth Harbour Cruising Club.

FAREHAM LAKE IS the NW arm and Portchester Lake is the NE arm from the junction with the main channel in Portsmouth Harbour. Both channels (which are 'lakes' only at high water) provide considerable reaches for sailing, though they are used principally by yachts of small or moderate size.

Fareham is situated round an ancient settlement at the ford where the present River Wallington joins the creek. It suffered greatly from the ravages of the Vikings but survived and was mentioned in the Domesday Book, under the name of Fernham, when it was credited with one church and two mills. In recent years Fareham has grown a great deal and is a very busy small market town carrying the main road traffic between Portsmouth, Gosport and Southampton.

Historically, Portchester is of greater importance because of its castle, with walls dating from Roman times and enclosing a Norman church in an area of about nine acres. Throughout the Napoleonic wars many French and Spanish prisoners were confined there. The castle remains in an excellent state of preservation, dominated by the enormous keep, added by the Normans, from which a magnificent view of the yacht anchorage and the harbour is obtained.

FAREHAM LAKE

This is the continuation of the main channel above Hardway, which has already been referred to, and the Reserve Dolphins on the opposite side. It is a wide, deep water channel as far as Bedenham Pier and is clearly marked by red piles on the port hand and green piles to starboard. The piles should not be approached closely as some are on the mud banks which are very steep in most parts, but the edge is shoaling into the channel between No 48 and No 49 starboard hand pile. Avoid steering from one pile direct to the next as the mud sometimes edges into the channel between them, and do not take the bends too sharply. Bedenham Pier is Admiralty property and must not be approached within 40ft (12.2m). A quarter mile beyond this pier on the opposite (starboard) side is the yacht yard of Wicor Marine Ltd, with long pier and pontoon off which there are many yacht moorings. Across from the pontoon is pile No 30A far up the mud which dries some 30ft inside it, and where many yachts go aground. The

Fareham Lake: Soundings in metres. Add 0.5m (1.8ft) at MLWS, 1.5m (5.0ft) at MLWN. Based on British Admiralty Chart No. 2631, with the permission of HM Stationery Office and of the Hydrographer of the Navy.

11.1. Reserve dolphins are to be left to starboard when sailing up Fareham Lake.

lake then takes a turn round Wicor Bend to the west into Heavy Reach where the channel becomes narrower and leads between extensive mud banks. This reach is marked by occasional piles, but these are well up on the mud. Pilotage is easiest at half tide, but can be confusing at high water when the mud flats are covered. The bottom is uneven, ranging from 8ft (2.4m) down to as little as 4ft (1.2m) in parts. Naval yacht moorings run west from the Naval pier on the south side and there are moorings for small yachts in shallower water on the north side.

At Power Station bend at the end of this reach the Lake (now a creek) turns to north and passes under power cables with a clearance of 64ft (19.5m), MHWS. The channel, which dries out at CD, then leads almost straight up to Fareham, edging to starboard a little under the trees about halfway up the reach. The mooring buoys here should be kept close under the port side, as they are on this side of the channel practically as far up as the quays.

A number of subsidiary creeks join Fareham Lake. Most of these dry out or are of little interest to visiting yachtsmen, but mention may be made of **Bomb Ketch Lake** and **Spider Lake**. As will be seen on the chart, these lie on the east side and enter Fareham Lake at the same point, the entrances being separated only by a spit of mud on which stands the G pile (No 54). This should be left well to port and another G pile (No 55) to starboard if entering Bomb Ketch Lake. This creek leads east and has about 8ft (2.4m) least water for a distance of 3 cables, except for a small 6ft (1.8m) patch in the middle of the entrance. A few yachts are moored in the entrance, but anchorage at the eastern end is exposed at HW and the bottom is foul, besides being within the Tipner firing area. Spider Lake is entered between No 53 R pile to port and No 54 G pile to starboard. It leads about NNE for ½ mile with a least depth of 6ft (1.8m), decreasing to 3ft (0.9m) east of Peewit Island, and the upper reach is within the area of the Tipner rifle range. These lakes are far from facilities, are isolated and abound with birds and shellfish, as also does Peewit Island. Old Naval cannon from Tipner range have been recovered at LWS. There are many private moorings in the main channel between Spider Lake and Wicor Marine.

Frater Lake on the west side of Fareham Lake leads to Bedenham Naval Quays where landing is prohibited. In **Cams Lake** there are two creeks leading to opposite corners of the bay. They dry out at LW.

Moorings, Anchorage and Facilities

Anchorage out of the fairway is possible in Fareham Lake anywhere above Bedenham Pier, except in the prohibited areas west of the two notice boards and between Salterns Quay and No 36 pile, as shown on the chart, or in the vicinity of moorings. It is necessary to use a trip line as the bottom is foul in many parts and a riding light is necessary because of shingle barges. Except at Hardway, referred to under Portsmouth, the best chance of obtaining the temporary use of a mooring is from the Wicor Marine Ltd, (Tel: Fareham 237112), who have many moorings for shoal draft yachts and a few yachts up to 6ft (1.8m) draft or more. Dry landing at pontoon at end of the long pier. Two slips and laying up and repairs undertaken. Chandlery, water and diesel, but far from shops.

Wicor Marine can launch from trailers craft of up to 7 tons displacement. Visiting yachts are welcome.

At Fareham small yachts have moorings. There is little water at LW springs but the bottom is soft mud and all except deep-keeled yachts will remain upright. Messrs R. & A. Hamper have a yacht building yard. Yachts of 6ft (1.8m) draft can proceed to the lower quay and yacht yard 2 hours either side of HW. Landing at pontoon at Fareham Sailing and Motor Boat Club, (Tel: Fareham 280738). Water on application. Fareham Yacht Harbour (Portsmouth Marine Engineering Ltd. (Tel: Fareham 232854) have pontoons at Lower Quay. Launching site at the public slipway nearby. Additional pontoons are planned (1986) at the Town Quay. There is an excellent shopping centre and pedestrian precinct not much more than ¼ mile walk away and public conveniences nearby. A hotel and restaurants in the town. EC Wednesday. Market day Monday.

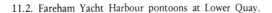

11.2. Fareham Yacht Harbour pontoons at Lower Quay.

11.3. Fareham Sailing and Motor Boat Club pontoon next to the Yacht Harbour.

11.4. Fareham Town Quay, which is being developed (1986).

PORTCHESTER LAKE

Portchester Lake provides a good sailing area as the channel is wide and deep in its centre as far as Tipner Lake, but in parts there is only 9 to 10ft (2.7 to 3.0m), and much less near the edges. In the reach up to Portchester Castle, the bottom is even more irregular. Thus, although with local knowledge or with the aid of the large-scale No 2631 Admiralty Chart, 6ft (1.8m) CD may be found up to the Castle and 1½ cables beyond it, a stranger may find as little as 2 to 4ft CD (0.6 to 1.2m) in some parts of the defined channel. It is well marked by numbered piles, red to port, green to starboard. However, some of these are well up on the mud or in shallow water, so they should not be approached closely nor (as in Fareham Lake) should a course be steered direct from one to the next at LW.

When approaching from Portsmouth Harbour, before coming to the Reserve Dolphins, the red pile No 57 will be seen which marks the west side of the entrance to the Creek. The first reach, Long Reach, is not quite straight, although its general direction is NE. Off the entrance to Tipner Lake at the end of the reach on the east side, the main channel takes a turn to the NW. Here care should be taken as shallow water extends far beyond the No 67 pile on the port hand and there is a drying shoal on the starboard side between No 80 and No 79 piles. Here the best water is on the port hand off No 68 and No 69 piles, but beyond the latter the deepest water lies mid-channel, leading northwards past Portchester Castle. In this reach there are four large spherical yellow buoys marking water to be left clear for Hovercraft when operating from Vosper's shipyard, further up the lake.

Off Portchester Castle and above it, the deep centre of the channel is much narrower and ends north of Horsea Island where the whole area is being reclaimed. Several creeks join Portchester Lake but, except for dinghy sailing, the only major one is Tipner Lake.

11.5. View from Portchester Castle keep over Portchester Lake to Tipner Lake and the motorway bridge.

Portchester Lake: Soundings in metres. Add 0.5m (1.8ft) at MLWS, 1.5m (5.0ft) at MLWN. Based on British Admiralty Chart No. 2631, with the permission of HM Stationery Officer and of the Hydrographer of the Navy.

Tipner Lake. This lake lies on the starboard side, where Portchester Lake turns westward about ½ mile south of Horsea Island. It is marked by channel posts, and the creek runs about easterly and passes through a prohibited anchorage before reaching Tipner Quays. Just before reaching these, there are drying moorings on the starboard side for shoal draft cruisers. Portsmouth Harbour Cruising Club has a landing at the drying concrete slip and water can be obtained at the club. On the port hand, opposite the quays, there is a small boat channel that links up with Langstone Harbour. After passing Tipner quays a smaller channel branches off on the starboard side and leads along under the shore to the end of the promenade. At half tide dinghies can land here, and it is only a short walk up the side-street to the buses which run to Portsmouth Guildhall.

Danger area. There is a danger area in Portchester Creek off Tipner Rifle Ranges which is shown on the chart and is defined by red notice boards. Red flags are flown at the Butts when firing is in progress, mostly at week-ends, and yachts are requested to make passage through the area as quickly as possible.

Port Solent. A major development of a marina-housing complex has started (1986) close to the M27/M275 motorway junction north of Horsea Island. The entrance to the 400-berth marina will be through a dredged channel and lock gates at the head of Porchester Lake.

Moorings, Anchorage and Facilities

The former anchorage, in rather poor holding ground in the channel south of the Castle, is now very limited as there are so many moorings that little room is left without encroaching upon the fairway. For the same reason, many of the yachts above the Castle are moored fore and aft so that they cannot swing into the fairway. Most of the moorings are licensed by the Portchester Sailing Club and let to their members. Application should be made to the duty officer of the club, which is helpful to visitors, to ascertain whether any moorings are temporarily vacant, but this cannot be counted on.

Landing at the north end of the Castle is made on the sailing club hard which has a concrete slip at the upper end. Yachts up to about 4½ft (1.4m) draft with their own legs can be scrubbed here with a 14ft (3.6m) tide, and it also provides a launching site. The sailing club is in the Old Vicarage, alongside the hard, (Tel: Cosham 376375). Water at tap near the Priory Church or on application at the club. There is a public car park and toilets about 100 yards from hard and the sailing club has its own car park. In the old village near the Castle is the Cormorant Inn and small shops, and ¾ mile up the road there are more shops, a PO, café, garage and bus stop. EC on Tuesday or for some shops Wednesday. The Castle is very well worth a visit.

12 Bembridge Harbour

High Water (Long): — 0h 5m Portsmouth.
Tidal Heights above datum: Outside the harbour approximately as at Portsmouth. Within harbour: MHWS 10.1ft (3.3m) MLWS (1.0ft) (0.3m) MHWN 7.6ft (2.3m) MLWN 1.3ft (0.4m)
Stream sets ½ mile E of St Helens Fort weakly to S at + 2h 0m Portsmouth, SE + 4h 0m, S + 6h 0m, NW — 3h 15m, W - 2h 0m, WSW + 1h 30m.
Depths: Most of the channel between the sands dries out at CD, except near the inner entrance. Within harbour itself, there is said to be a minimum depth of 1m in the channel from No. 10 buoy to the marina.
Yacht Clubs: Bembridge SC, Brading Haven YC.

BEMBRIDGE HARBOUR OR Brading Haven, as it used to be known, is the most easterly of the Island harbours. It is a natural formation sheltered from the prevailing winds and with good facilities. The wide clean sands in the approach, fishing and shrimping and walks to the Foreland make Bembridge a good centre for the family yachtsman. In the days of sail St Helens Road provided an anchorage for the assembly of British fleets, and water casks were filled from a spring at Bembridge. The Road was the scene of the Spithead mutiny in 1797.

The disadvantage is that the entrance channel and the harbour itself are so shallow that they are suitable only for shallow draft yachts except near HW. However, the Bembridge Harbour Improvement Company Limited, who bought all harbour rights from British Railways, are gradually improving the yachting amenities.

The Approach and Entrance

The approach to Bembridge is via the yellow beacon (*Fl Y 2s 1M*) situated about 3 cables NW of St Helens Fort (*Fl (3) 10s*). There is a tide guage on the beacon which indicates the depth of water over the shallowest section of the channel, which is in the vicinity of Nos 6 and 8 buoys. The beacon is painted yellow and has a yellow saltire top-mark fitted. The entrance to the channel is about 2 cables to the SSW and is marked by two buoys, No 01 conical G to starboard and No 2 R can further on to port. They are not very big - see photograph. From here on the course to be taken is marked by green conical buoys with odd numbers to starboard and by red can buoys with even numbers to port. Their position is altered to suit the changing course of the channel and is only approximately shown on the chartlet. The channel becomes narrower and deeper as No 11 starboard hand buoy is approached. Ahead lies a pool where many club boats lie at moorings. To the east may be seen the conspciuous buildings of the erstwhile Royal Spithead Hotel and the Bembridge Sailing Club.

The main channel to Bembridge Marina at St Helen's Quay leads in a westerly direction and is marked on the starboard side by Nos 11A, 13, 15 and 17 G conical buoys and on the port side by Nos 10A, 12, 12A, 14 and 16 R can buoys.

Bembridge Harbour: Soundings in metres. Add 0.03 m (0.1 ft) at MLWS, 0.4 m (1.3 ft) at MLWN. Based on Bembridge Harbour Improvement Co Ltd plan and on British Admiralty Chart No. 2050, with the permission of HM Stationery Office and of the Hydrographer of the Navy and of the Bembridge Harbour Improvement Co.

12.1. St. Helens Fort, now privately owned.

12.2. Bembride approach beacon and tide gauge.

12.3. No. 01 G conical buoy. The first of the starboard hand marks.

12.4. The second starboard hand mark is No. 1, seen here with St Helens Sea Mark in the backround.

The harbour is administered by the Bembridge Harbour Improvements Co Ltd. General Manager (in which the position of Harbour Master is vested) - Major S. C. Selwyn MBE (Tel: IoW 872828).

Lights: The only permanent light is the *Fl Y 2s 1M* light on the beacon at the entrance.

Anchorage, Moorings and Facilities

The best anchorage outside the harbour is at Under Tyne off the Bembridge SC starting line, less than ½ mile east of the former Royal Spithead Hotel. This position is well protected from winds from south to west, though exposed if the wind veers to NW and other directions. Anchor outside the permanent moorings in sufficient depth of water and buoy the anchor. The hard shown on the chart is more in the nature of a landing place between the rocks but at HW land on the beach whence follow the shore to Bembridge.

A number of visitors' berths are available at the marina, where only one or two feet of water can be expected at LW, but below is soft mud and craft up to 6 feet draught usually remain upright. Accommodation at the marina is very limited on Saturday nights and during the holiday period, so it is advisable to get in as early as possible on the tide leaving a margin for departure if necessary. Berthing Master - Mr R. (Bob) Green (Tel: IoW 872973).

Craft that can take the ground are permitted to anchor fore-and-aft on the beach immediately to port on entering the inner harbour if there is space available. Anchoring elsewhere in the harbour is prohibited.

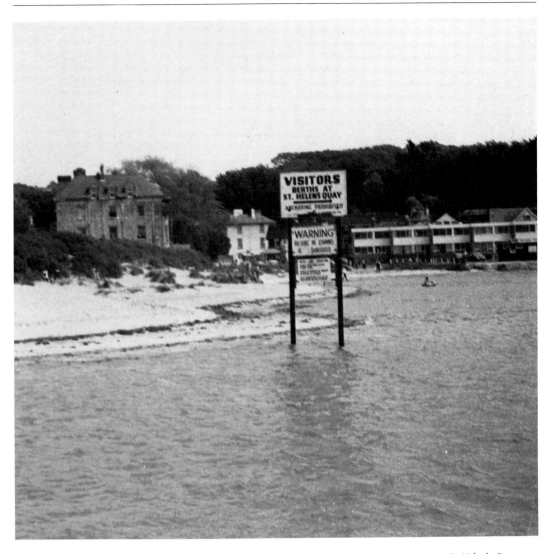

12.5. Facing east showing the steep bank on the port hand and the notice board directing visitors to St Helen's Quay.

There is some visitors' accommodation at the Bembridge Boatyard Ltd pontoon (Tel: IoW 872423) and drying moorings may be available from A. A. Coombes (Tel: IoW 872296) or from Attrill's Yard (Tel: IoW 872319).

The Brading Haven YC adjoins the Quay and temporary members are welcomed. There are small shops and The Hayloft restaurant (Tel: IoW 872014) at St Helens ¼ mile distant up the hill. EC varies but PO Saturdays. Bembridge itself is nearly ¾ mile along the south harbour. Here there are hotels, restaurants and shops. EC Thursday.

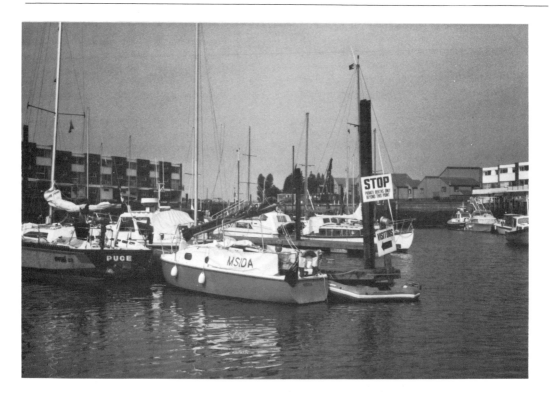

12.6. Bembridge Marina visitors' pontoons.

Bembridge is an active racing centre with several yacht yards: Attrill's and Duver on the St Helens side of the harbour and Coombes, TT Boat Designs and Bembridge Boatyard Ltd on the south side. Chandlery at Coombes and yacht yards. Diesel fuel may be obtained from Bembridge Boatyard Ltd, from K. Stratton beside the marina and, subject to their own needs, from the jetties and pontoons off Attrill's and Duver's yards. Petrol can be had from Bembridge Motor Services Ltd, next to Bembridge Boatyard Ltd. Launching sites: concrete ramp near St Helen's Church seamark (for about 3 hours either side of HW), and from sands and beaches, or by arrangement with yacht yards or at clubs by permission only. Buses to Ryde and all parts of the Island.

13 Langstone Harbour

High Water: + 0h 5m Portsmouth.
Tidal Heights above datum: Approx MHWS 15.8ft (4.8m) MLWS 2.1ft (0.6m) MHWN 12.7ft (3.9m) MLWN 5.9ft (1.8m).
Stream sets in Hayling Bay rotary anti-clockwise 075° at about + 5h 45m Portsmouth; 360° at — 4h 0m; 315° at — 2h 0m; 280° at HW; 260° at + 1h 0m; 230° at + 2h 0m; 160° at + 2h 30m; 130° at + 4h 0m; 110° at + 5h 30m. Streams weak with maximum 0.9 knot HW to + 1h 0m and 0.7 knot — 5h 0m.
Depths: The depth of water on the inner Langstone Bar varies from time to time and has been about 6ft (1.8m) at CD, with as little as 2ft (0.6m) outside on the southern hook of the East Winner. Within the harbour there are reaches with 6ft (1.8m) and more - see chart.
Yacht Clubs: Locks SC, Tudor SC, Eastney Cruising Association.

LANGSTONE HAS ALWAYS been a somewhat neglected harbour and during the French wars it was much used as a retreat for privateers seeking to avoid pursuit in the English Channel. The inhabitants of Hayling Island were once well known for smuggling and wrecking. 'Mulberry Harbours' were made in Langstone Harbour in preparation for the assault on the beaches of Normandy in June 1944. The plan was for a harbour, built in sections, to be towed across and sunk on the French shore. There were several hundred of these concrete units made; one ran aground on the Sinah Sands, broke it's back and remains as a monument to a remarkable achievement.

The days of privateers, smugglers and other colourful characters have passed but the lonely backwaters which they frequented still remain. There are creeks where the only sound comes from the seabirds, and reaches in the Langstone Channel where it is still possible to find room for cruising yachts to anchor in 6ft (1.8m) and over, though far from shore facilities. The harbour provides a good cruising area for dinghy sailing and there is plenty of active small boat racing.

The bar and the Winner sands, on which innumerable vessels have been driven ashore, have given the approach a bad reputation, but in normal summer weather and on the flood tide the entrance presents no particular problems. It is, in fact, easier than Chichester Harbour entrance.

The Approach and Entrance

The approach from the Solent presents no difficulties. Hold a course past the Horse Sand Fort to clear the nearby shoal shown on the chart and the submerged barrier. Then steer NE to bring the Horse Sand Fort into line astern with Noman's Land Fort, whence keep on this transit steering 055°. This leads (in the direction of the prominent Royal Hotel almost midway on the front of Hayling Island) to Langstone RW Fairway buoy (*L Fl 10s*), distance about 2¼ miles. A beacon marking a dangerous wreck will be left to port and an obstruction (4ft at CD) is left to starboard. If there is fog take care not to overstand the Langstone buoy. Note: the wreck beacon is shown on the charts as having a top-mark of two spheres vertical, but the top-mark is usually missing.

13.1. The dolphin marking the south side of the main passage through the submerged barrier between Southsea and Horse Sand Fort.

13.2. The boat passage through the submerged barrier between Southsea and the Horse Sand Fort going west. South Parade just beyond the opening.

13.3. The wreck BRB (F1(2) 5s) between Horse Sand Fort and Langstone Fairway buoy, less it's topmark (see text).

13.4. Langstone Fairway buoy RW (L F1 10s).

If proceeding from Portsmouth the short cut may be taken through the gap in the barrier marked by a pile on an obstruction on the north side and a dolphin (QR) on the south. This carries 4ft (1.2m) CD. Then steer 079° for Langstone buoy heading midway between the conspicuous hotel and Eastoke Pt. The course leaves the wreck to starboard and leads just north of Langstone buoy. Alter course when it is sighted to leave it to port. There is also a second passage known as the 'Boat Passage' through the submerged barrier. This lies close inshore and is marked by beacons (see photograph). The depth is only 3ft (0.9m) CD, and 2ft (0.6m) east of it.

Approaching from the eastward the hook-shaped extension of the East Winner extends over 1½ miles from the shore, with depths as little as 2ft (0.6m) CD, at its extremity off which lies the East Winner South cardinal buoy (yellow/black unlit). These shoals (which frequently shift after gales and tend to lengthen) may be cleared in about 6ft (1.8m) CD, by keeping Haslar hospital open southward of Southsea Castle, until the Fairway buoy comes into line with the east side of Langstone harbour entrance. Then steer for the buoy leaving it to port. Here the in-going stream begins + 5h 40m Portsmouth to the NE, gradually turning anti-clockwise to end WNW at high water. The maximum spring rate of 1.2 knots, direction 325° from − 2h 0m for an hour. The out-going begins to the south at + 1h 20m and attains maximum spring rate 2.1 knots S by E at + 3h 0m, ending easterly. The streams tend to follow the channel when the sands are uncovered and are stronger as the entrance, which is very deep, is approached. Here a spring rate of 3.5 knots is attained in the entrance on the flood (but there is an hour's slack at about half tide) and 4½ knots (sometimes more) on the ebb which begins at + 0h 25m Portsmouth.

From the Fairway Buoy a course should be steered to the middle of the entrance between the sands, allowing for any athwartship tide. Alternatively, bring the beacons on the two dolphins on the west side of the entrance into line at about 344° and follow this transit, bearing to starboard ¼ mile before reaching the entrance, when the channel is obvious.

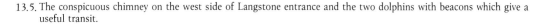

13.5. The conspicuous chimney on the west side of Langstone entrance and the two dolphins with beacons which give a useful transit.

Entrance of Langstone Harbour: Soundings in metres. Add 0.6 m (2.1 ft) at MLWS, 1.8 m (5.9 ft) at MLWN. Based on British Admiralty Chart No. 3418, with the permission of HM Stationery Office and of the Hydrographer of the Navy.

The easiest time of approach in good weather is on the young flood before the East Winner (which is fairly steep-to) is covered so that the direction of the channel can be seen. At this state of the tide the East or West Winner afford some protection to the channel except during onshore winds. Nearer high tide there is of course more water and the East Winner can often be identified by the seas breaking on the sands: in bad weather they are covered by a mass of breaking water. During strong onshore winds and gales Langstone Harbour should not be approached as the seas break on the bar and in the shoal water far south of the Fairway buoy. The East Winner is a lee shore in south and SW winds; on the ebb tide under gale conditions it is particularly dangerous. Even in good weather entry on the ebb should be avoided if possible owing to the strength of the stream in and near the entrance.

At the top of the narrows at the entrance, pontoons for the ferries will be seen on either hand, and once past these the harbour widens out into a tidal lake over 2 miles across, congested with sand and mud banks, but intersected with channels and small creeks.

Gunnery Practice: There is a rifle range at Eastney, with danger area SW towards the gap in the Barrier. The Fraser Gunnery Range, covering approaches to Langstone and Chichester harbours, is at Eastney Point SW of the chimney. **Danger Signals** displayed 30m before and while firing. Large red flag above International Pendant 1 for **area 1** (200 yards 120° to 200°). Above Pendant 2 for **area 2** (6000 yards 120° to 155°). Above Pendant 3 for **area 3** (12,500 yards 120° to 155°). Above Pendant 4 for **area 4** (24,000 yards 126° to 146°). Areas 2, 3 and 4 with lethal ammunition. Signals displayed from range building, SW corner South Parade Pier, W side Langstone entrance, Harbour Master's Office and Selsey CG. Naval Patrol boat, flying red flag is stationed close to danger areas when areas 2, 3 and 4 in use. Normal hours 1300-1530 Monday to Friday, but forenoon used when weather on previous days unsuitable.

Lights: After rounding the Fairway buoy *L Fl 10s*, the entrance can usually be seen at night against the lights on Portsdown Hill and there is a *Q R* light on the outer beacon at the entrance and another *Fl R* 4 cables north also on the west side. Within the harbour there is a light on the port hand E Milton buoy *Fl (4) R 10s* and opposite on the starboard hand NW Sinah buoy *Fl G 5s*. These lights assist in the approach channel. There is also a light *VQR* in the Broom Channel at the entrance of Salterns Lake. In the Langstone Channel there is a lit buoy ALPHA *QR* and two lit beacons *Fl G 3s* and *Fl R 3s*.

THE MAIN CHANNEL AND HARBOUR

Within the entrance the main channel, which runs in a northerly direction, is wide and deep. On the west side it is joined at the entrance by Eastney Lake and on the east by Sinah Lake. Northward of these creeks the channel is very wide and there are many orange mooring buoys in deep water on the port side and an increasing number on the starboard hand in the vicinity of the concrete Mulberry grounded on the west of Sinah Sands. About 1½ cables beyond this is the previously mentioned green conical starboard hand NW Sinah buoy, and on the opposite side the red port hand E Milton buoy. The deepest water is on the west side of the channel. There is plenty of water in the fairway marked for the dredgers between the two light buoys, though there is a small 1ft (0.3m) shoal about 2 cables south of the NW Sinah buoy.

Beyond these buoys the Langstone Channel, which is deep for nearly two miles, branches off to the NE but the main channel continues northward for another ½ mile before branching into the Broom Channel which continues NW to the road embankment north of Portsea Island.

Perches within the harbour have a high casualty rate due to oyster dredging and many are either missing altogether or are without their top-mark.

Owing to the number of moorings and the narrow fairway left for the gravel dredgers and ships proceeding to Kendall's Wharf, there is no room left for anchoring in the main channel. Anchorage is now only practicable in the Langstone Channel and Russell's Lake but — see below - shallow draft yachts such as twin-keelers or multi-hullers can explore and find anchorages out of the fairways and in minor creeks not available to yachts of deeper draft.

Moorings, Anchorage and Facilities

There are six visitors' moorings for temporary use on the east side of the entrance, south of the notice board indicating where the cables cross. The position is exposed and very uncomfortable in high winds. In case of SE winds of much strength there is said to be a danger of these moorings dragging off the shelf and into the deep water of the channel; the ebb could then take one out to the Winner, mooring and all! It is best to go ashore to consult the Harbour Master who will advise whether any of the numerous moorings in the harbour are available for a longer stay and give any other information required. The Harbour Master, Mr H. J. Owen has his office nearby on the Hayling side of the ferry (Tel: Hayling Island 463419). VHF watch on Channel 16, call sign "LANGSTONE HARBOUR OFFICE": working channel 12. Also see Langstone Marina p. 114.

Water skiing is permitted only with a licence from the Harbour Office and within certain specified areas. One such area is marked with yellow buoys and perches over the shoal sands either side of the Langstone Channel. There is a speed limit of 10 knots other than in the water skiing areas.

13.6. The Harbour Master's office (large building with flag-staff in front) and *Ferryboat Inn*. Launching site between. One of the visitors' moorings in foreground.

13.7. The stranded concrete 'mulberry' marked as "concrete structure" on some charts on the east side of the harbour. There is shallow water to the south of it and a shoal about a cable west and beyond.

Sinah Lake

Sinah Lake is on the Hayling Island side just within the entrance. All the best positions are occupied by moorings as is the Kench, the small bay on the south side, which dries out at low water.

It is best to enter Sinah Lake close to the ferry pontoon where there is 1ft (0.3m) CD whereas farther northward the sands dry out over a cable south of the Mulberry. Care should be taken to avoid being set against the ferry pontoon where the stream is strong, especially on the ebb 2 hours after HW when it attains nearly 5 knots at springs. The channel runs at first in a NE by E direction and deepens to over a fathom north of the Kench. There is an inner bar which dries out as shown on the chart, and then a ½ mile reach to E and NE with depths ranging from 8ft (2.4m) down to 3ft (0.9m) CD at the eastern end. There are few marks to aid pilotage in the western part of Sinah Lake other than the yachts on moorings which show the trend of the channel, but some of these are shallow draft so keep close to the line of the larger yachts. The upper reaches are perched and lead to the Rod Rythe creek (which joins Sinah Lake to the Langstone Channel) and is also marked by perches. This provides a short cut which can be used by dinghies and shallow craft and is stated locally to be navigable by yachts at about half tide.

There is no room available in Sinah Lake for anchoring, so the visiting yachtsman should apply to the Harbour Master at Ferry Point for the use of a vacant mooring if any is available.

At Sinah there is the Ferry Boat Inn, and a café which supplies stores in summer. Water point behind Inn, or from Boat-harbour Company opposite Inn who also supply fuel. Harbour Master's office and workshop adjacent. Launching site on slip. Car park nearby. Bus service to Hayling Village in summer, where there are hotels, shops and PO. EC Wednesday. Frequent ferries in daylight hours to Eastney, thence summer bus service to Southsea. Fuel and water from the Harbour Board premises.

Eastney Lake (or the Locks) and Langstone Marina

This shallow lake lies just inside the entrance of Langstone Harbour on the west side, opposite Sinah Lake. To enter the lake an incoming vessel should pass between the Ferry Pontoon and the first Royal Marine mooring buoy. Then the buoy should be kept straight on her stern, and course steered almost west (Mag), in the passage between the craft moored on each side of the creek. This creek should be approached with *caution* as the channel is narrow and is congested with moorings for small craft. There is another channel running south just inside the Ferry point, at the entrance to Eastney Lake, but it is very shallow. The former of these two creeks has a lead south to an important new (1986) development, Langstone Marina. The marina basin has been constructed to accommodate 300 berths. A dredged channel is planned to provide access at all states of the tide, and there is to be a 'holding bay', with mooring posts, for craft waiting for sufficient water to pass the entrance gate, which will have an automatic sill, retaining about 1.8m of water in the marina basin.

The Locks Sailing Club house is situated at Milton Locks on the north side of Eastney Lake; it is an active club and holds numerous dinghy races during the summer. There is a hard just north of the locks, and a general stores up the road. EC Wednesday. Easy connections with Southsea and Portsmouth. Launching site at end of road near Ferry pontoon.

Milton or Velder Lake is the next shallow creek north of Eastney Lake on the west side of the main channel, but is of little significance as it leads only to an area of reclaimed land.

13.8. Model of Langstone Marina at the south of Easteney Lake.

Broom Channel

This continuation of the main channel in a NW direction to Hillsea is used by ballast dredgers as far as Kendall's Wharf. It is comparatively narrow but carries 7ft (2.1m) of water for the first ½ mile, though it shoals quickly about 2 cables south of Kendall's Wharf and dries out at chart datum a cable beyond. It is marked by perches on the mud on either side and 3 buoys. The Tudor Sailing Club is situated at the northern end of this channel near the road bridge

Langstone Harbour: Soundings in metres. Add 0.6 m (2.1 ft) at MLWS, 1.8 m (5.9 ft) at MLWN. Based on British Admiralty Chart No. 3418, with the permission of HM Stationery Office and of the Hydrographer of the Navy.

and has many moorings for shallow draft craft. Half a mile to the south is the Portsmouth Sailing Centre.

There is no room for anchoring in the deeper part of Broom Channel below Kendall's Wharf as the fairway is used by the ballast dredgers. Apply to the Tudor SC (Tel: Portsmouth 662002) to ascertain whether a visitor's mooring is available, preferably at neaps when there is more water.

Russell's Lake joins Broom Channel on the east side and runs between mud flats to Farlington Marshes. It is only 1ft (0.3m) CD in the entrance but is wide and has deeper pools with from 5ft (1.5m) to 10ft (3.0m). It is marked by occasional perches. The pools provide quiet, though rather remote, anchorages.

Saltern's Lake lies on the west side of the Broom Channel. It has a red buoy *VQR* at the entrance and perches mark the channel. It is no longer used by ballast dredgers and is largely filled by yacht moorings.

13.9. East Milton buoy (*Fl (4) R 10s*) looking south-west. Beacon *BRB* behind.

13.10. The R buoy Salterns (*VQR*) at the entrance to Salterns Lake. Great Salterns Quay in the background.

13.11. Kendall's Wharf near the head of Broom Channel.

LANGSTONE CHANNEL

The entrance of this channel lies northward of the Sinah sands and the NW Sinah green conical light buoy. There is a middle ground in the entrance with as little as 1ft (0.3m) CD and a wreck marked by a beacon with two black spheres. The easiest entry is south of this shoal, approaching from the NW Sinah buoy and treating the wreck beacon and four moored Admiralty rafts as port hand marks. Leave to starboard the metal structures which are well up on Sinah sands.

The channel is wide and deep, ranging from 18 to 9ft (5.5 to 2.7m) for the first mile. It runs in a NE direction and is marked by occasional perches. The yellow buoys are water skiing marks, sometimes in shallow water, and are of no navigational significance though they may help to indicate the general direction of the channel. About a mile from the entrance there is a red lit buoy ALPHA (*QR*) and an accompanying unlit starboard hand green buoy ROD. The channel turns north to another green starboard buoy STOKE and two lit beacons *Fl R 3s* and *Fl G 3s* that mark the dredged channel to Havant Quay.

13.12. The first of the four Admiralty rafts in Langstone Channel, looking back to the wreck beacon *BRB*.

13.13. The R buoy Alpha (*QR*) about a mile up the Langstone Channel.

13.14. The unlit G buoy Rod, that marks the east side of the channel opposite Alpha.

13.15. The small G buoy Bridge at the entrance to North Lake.

13.16. Havant Quay at the North end of the Langstone Channel.

North Lake and South Lake both dry out and lead easterly through the gap in the former railway bridge to Hayling road bridge. North Lake is the better marked of the two and navigable with sufficient rise of tide if proceeding to Chichester Harbour. A green buoy BRIDGE provides a starboard mark at the entrance to North Lake, but although the charts indicate 'marked by perches' there were none seen in 1986. The road bridge can only be passed under by craft without masts as there is no more than 7ft (2.1m) clearance below it at high water springs and the stream is strong. The span of the bridge with the best water under it is marked on the pile on the north side with a black diamond on a white background with black bands below it and by a black triangle on the south side. For Langstone village see Chichester Harbour.

There is plenty of room to anchor in Langstone Channel, which is quiet except in strong winds against the tide or when water skiing is in progress. The best holding ground is on the north side beyond the rafts, little more than a mile from the Locks SC which is not far by dinghy with outboard engine in ordinary weather. However, it is important to anchor well clear of the channel, as the dredgers that ply to Havant Quay have, it is said, scant respect for anchored yachts.

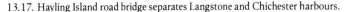

13.17. Hayling Island road bridge separates Langstone and Chichester harbours.

14 Chichester Harbour

High Water: At entrance + 0h 5m Portsmouth.

Tidal Heights above datum: Entrance MHWS 16.2ft (4.9m) MLWS 2.3ft (0.7m) MHWN 13ft (3.9m) MLWN 6ft (1.8m).

Stream sets to westward 2.1 miles S of Cakeham Tower at 1 knot maximum — 2h 0m Portsmouth. Begins about NW rotating anti-clockwise to finish S, and easterly stream begins + 5h 0m Portsmouth. For Hayling Bay see Langstone Harbour.

Depths: Bar dredged to 5ft (1.5m) CD giving over 6ft at MLWS, but depths and sands vary from time to time. Channel at entrance very deep. Inner bar NE of the NW Winner Buoy 5ft (1.5m) to 7ft (2.1m). In Chichester Channel depths vary from 9ft (2.7m) upwards as far as Itchenor.

Yacht Clubs: Birdham YC, Bosham SC, Chichester YC, Emsworth SC, Emsworth Cruising Association, Emsworth Slipper SC, Dell Quay SC, Hayling Island SC, Itchenor SC, Langstone SC, Mengham Rythe SC, Thorney Island SC (RAF), West Wittering SC.

CHICHESTER IS ONE of the largest and most concentrated yachting centres in the South of England. This is not surprising as it provides a cruising area in itself, with several miles of sheltered water in its four main channels: Emsworth, Thorney, Bosham and Chichester. Besides this, all the creeks and harbours of the Solent are within easy reach and it is a good point for departure to France or more extended cruises. It is also a great centre for dinghy and other racing. Within the harbour there is a speed limit of 6 knots for yachts under power.

Historically, the harbour has associations deeply rooted in the past for it was known to Roman, Saxon and Dane. At one time there was a monastery in the village of Bosham and the largest bell was seized and carried away by the Danes on one of their numerous raids. Legend has it that no sooner had the raiders departed than the monks returned to the belfry and began a peal. The missing note came ringing over the water from the Danish vessel, over a mile away in Bosham Deep; then the bottom of the raider's ship opened, the bell sank, and the planks of their vessel closed together again. According to the legend the bell could only be recovered by a team of pure white heifers. Today, a replica of the bell is seen on the burgees of members of the Bosham Sailing Club in all parts of the harbour, but, to date, the team of white heifers has remained lacking.

The Approach, Bar and Entrance

There are extensive shoals off the entrance to Chichester, and large parts dry out at low water. On the west side there are the West Pole sands, which have extended south as far as the Bar Beacon (see chartlet). On the east side the Middle Pole and the East Pole sands extend nearly 1½ miles off the shore. A depth of 2m at MLWS can be expected at the bar, but after gales the bottom can vary by 0.75m either way. An incoming yacht must wait for sufficient rise of tide to cross the bar with an adequate factor of safety, especially in rough weather or a swell. In normal weather with reasonable visibility there is no difficulty about approach and entry

14.1. Chichester bar beacon.   14.2. The small R can buoy some 800m   14.3. West Winner beacon (*QG*) and tide
                                south of the Bar Beacon (see text)   gauge.

after half flood, but the ebb attains a spring rate of well over 5 knots at the entrance. A yacht under sail cannot make headway against this unless she has a commanding wind or auxiliary power. In common with all shoaling lee shores, extra care should be taken if approaching with onshore winds or swell. The approach is dangerous in thick weather and extremely so with strong or southerly gale force winds against an ebb tide.

When approaching from east or west keep well offshore (according to the height of the tide and weather conditions) until the clump of trees at Eastoke Point (see photograph) on the west side of the entrance and Chichester Bar Beacon (*Fl W R 5s 14m*) have been identified, when approach can then be made from due south. The Chichester Harbour Conservancy was, in 1986, considering a permanent landfall mark south of the Bar Beacon and as a temporary measure established an unlit red can buoy in position 194°, 800m from the Bar Beacon to encourage mariners to give the west Pole tail a wider berth (this buoy is marked on the chartlet). Leave the beacon half a cable to port and shape a course to pass midway between Eastoke and West Winner Beacons. On this course a minimum depth of water of 1.4 metres at CD will be found just abreast the Chichester Bar Beacon. Shallow patches exist to the east and west of the approach course. Under low water conditions deep draft vessels approaching from the west and southeast should steer courses to arrive at a point at least one mile south of Chichester Bar Beacon before altering course to the northward. This will avoid the shallow patches of the West and East Pole sands. The Chichester Bar Beacon bears a tide gauge which

120

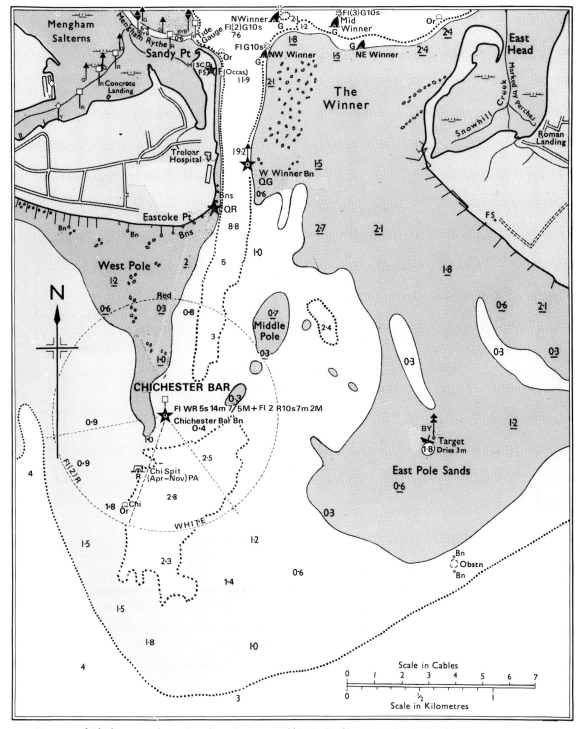

Entrance of Chichester Harbour: Soundings in metres. Add 0.7m (2.3ft) at MLWS, 1.8m (6.0ft) at MLWN. Based on British Admiralty Chart No. 3418, with the permission of HM Stationery Office and of the Hydrographer of the Navy.

The many channels are liberally marked by perches bearing port, starboard and cardinal top-marks as appropriate. Not all can be shown on this chartlet. The perches and their top-marks have a high casualty rate and one should expect some to be missing.

14.4. Eastoke Point and conspicuous trees.

indicates the depth of water above CD, thus if it reads 1.0 metres there will be a depth of 2.4 metres half a cable to the east of it.

When the bar has been crossed, the depths slowly increase to 9ft (2.7m) when ¼ mile off the entrance and at least a depth of 30ft (9.0m) in the entrance.

As the entrance is approached, it will be seen that there are three groynes, with drum-topped beacons on their seaward ends, to be left well to port, as they dry 5ft (1.5m) and a fourth which has the Eastoke Beacon (Q R) on it. This beacon should be left ¼ to ½ cable to port and beyond it are three more beacons, all to be left to port as the yacht comes into the entrance.

In the entrance channel itself the deepest water lies in the centre of the channel but there is also plenty of water on the west side as the beach is fairly steep-to. The whole of the area east of the entrance channel is choked by a big shingle bank, the Winner, extending over ½ mile from the eastern shore. As the yacht comes to the entrance, Treloar's Hospital will be prominent on the port side, and the channel lies between the shore and the West Winner Beacon (Q G) which is to be left to starboard. Continuing along the western shore, Hayling Island Sailing Club, standing on Sandy Point at the northern end, will be left to port, and 3 cables NE of it lies the green conical buoy, the NW Winner (Fl G 10s).

Chichester Bar Radio Beacon
Call sign - CH
Frequency - 303.4 Khz

This radio beacon, located on the Bar Beacon itself, transmits in a 6-minute sequence signals which give the wind direction and force at the Bar. The call sign sequence is transmitted during minutes 1 and 4 of the 6-minute cycles, as follows:

```
CH   CH   CH   CH
4 second dash
1 to 8 dashes          (indicating wind direction)
4 second dash
0 to 8 dots            (indication wind force)
12 second dash
CH   CH
5 second silence
2 minute silence
```

The wind information is given as:

Direction at the start of the transmission, clockwise, one dash being NE: eight dashes being N.

Speed in Beaufort notation averaged over the previous 3 minutes, the number of dots indicate the lower limit of the force number. No dots indicate zero wind.

Lights: There is a *Fl WR 5s 14m 7/5M + Fl (2) R 10s 7m 2M* light on the Chichester Bar Beacon. Keep well off shore until in the 120° white sector of this light. Approach in the white sector after sufficient rise of tide. The beacon on the groyne carries a *QR* light, while that on the W Winner Beacon shows *Q G*. These are followed by the NW Winner buoy showing *Fl G 10s* which is left to starboard, by when Fishery buoy's *Q (6) + LFl 15s* south cardinal light will be seen.

The Emsworth channel is well lit with NW Pilsey buoy showing *Fl G 5s*: Verner beacon (*Fl R 10s*): Marker beacon (*Fl (2) G 10s*) and the two beacons, NE Hayling (*Fl (2) R 10s*) and Emsworth beacon (*Q (6) + L Fl 15s*). Up Sweare Deep the Sweare Deep beacon shows *Fl (3) R 10s* and the Northney beacon at the entrance to the Northney Marina channel will show *Fl (4) R 10s*. The marina itself is well lit by pontoon lights and will be quite apparent. The northerly channel to Emsworth and the Emsworth Yacht Harbour is lit by Fisherman's beacon showing *Fl (3) R 10s* and beyond, Echo beacon with *Fl (3) G 10s*.

The Chichester channel is similarly well lit as far as Itchenor: The N Winner (*Fl (2) G 10s*), Mid Winner (*Fl (3) G 10s*) buoys and the East Head beacon (*Fl (4) G 10s*) mark the starboard side of the channel, while Stocker (*Fl (3) R 10s*), Sandhead (*Fl (4) R 10s*) and NE Sandhead (*Fl R 10s*) buoys mark the port hand and northerly side. From here will be seen the Camber beacon with the south cardinal light *Q (6) + L Fl 15s* marking the division of the Thorney and Chichester channels.

In the Thorney channel the Pilsey Island beacon (*Gp Fl (2) R 10s*) marks the port side of the gap in the first line of broken piles and a further beacon showing *Fl G 5s* marks the starboard side of the gap in the second line of broken piles.

The Chichester channel continues lit by the Chaldock beacon (*Gp Fl (2) G 10s*) and Fairway buoy (*Gp Fl. (3) G 10s*). The Harbourmaster's pontoon at Itchenor is lit by *2 FG* (vert). After this there are only the Birdham beacon (*Gp Fl (4) G 10s*) and the CYB beacon (*Fl G 5s*) that mark the channels to the Birdham Yacht Basin and the Chichester Yacht Basin respectively.

14.5. Fishery south cardinal buoy (Q(6) +   14.7. Camber Beacon.   14.8. Roman Transit.
L Fl 15s)

THE CHICHESTER CHANNEL

The directions will have brought the yacht within the entrance off Sandy Point and course altered to starboard to pass between the N Winner buoy (starboard) and the Fishery buoy to port. There is something in the nature of an inner bar extending from the N Winner buoy to the west end of the drying part of the Stocker's Sand. The least water is 7ft (2.1m) except for a 5ft (1.5m) CD patch about ½ cable NE of the N Winner buoy. The course then becomes almost due east and the channel soon deepens. It leads between the Stocker Sand on the north side - steep-to and dries 6ft (1.8m) in parts - and the Winner Sand on the south. The former is marked by the red can Stocker (Fl (3) R 10s) and Copyhold port hand buoys and the latter by the Mid-Winner (Fl (3) G 10s) and NE Winner starboard hand green conical buoys. After passing between the Copyhold and NE Winner buoys the channel bears to the NE, leaving the sandy promontory of East Head to starboard and the Sandhead red can buoy (Fl (4) R 10s) to port.

After passing the latter buoy a very conspicuous distant clump of trees called Stoke Clump will be seen (except in hazy weather) to the NE and in the nearest distance, about 1½ miles away, will be seen a wooded shore. The correct course up the next reach of Chichester Channel is held by keeping Stoke Clump over the middle of the trees on the wooded shore and on with a white rectangular beacon on the foreshore 3 cables west of Cobnor point at 032° (see photograph). If Stoke Clump is obscured there is Roman Transit Beacon in foreground which can be used. It is best to steer on a transit because some of the perches on the starboard hand in this reach are far up on the mud, which extends over ¼ mile from the shore and is covered near high water, creating a hazard on which many yachts run aground. The Transit leads close to the Camber, south cardinal beacon (Q (6) + L Fl 15s) situated on the NE side of the entrance to the Thorney Channel. This should be left to port and, continuing

032°

14.6. In the distance Stoke Clump is over the middle of the trees and the Roman Transit beacon in transit at 032°.

up the main channel, the broken piles and stumps of the old proposed embankment will lie well up on the mud beyond the port hand perches the whole way to Cobnor.

Towards the end of this reach at the Chaldock beacon (Fl (2) G 10s) the channel bears to the east and the beacon is rounded leaving it on the starboard hand, as the mud extends nearly 3 cables from the shore with two measured distance beacons with triangle tops high up on it. The channel then runs south of Cobnor Point leaving the Deep End beacon and the entrance to Bosham Channel to port and passing the green conical Fairway buoy (Fl (3) G 10s) on either side as it is in deep water. South of the buoy is another pair of measured distance beacons, 3040ft from the first pair. The channel turns about ESE into the Itchenor Reach, and is wide and well marked. This reach leads past Itchenor, a charming village of red-stoned houses and cottages on the south side. The fairway is crowded by lines of yachts on moorings but a passage is left between them.

The channel continues for nearly a mile beyond Itchenor before bending round Longmore Point (off which the channel is marked by several red can perches) to a north and then more north-easterly direction. The reach beyond this is not nearly so well marked and can only be navigated with sufficient rise of tide. As far as the entrance to Birdham Pool there is 1ft (0.3m) CD, but the mud extends a long way from the southern shore and the best water is on the northern side.

The creek leading to Birdham Pool and Chichester Canal is entered by leaving Birdham Bn (Fl (4) G 10s) to port and a series of BW perches to starboard. The dredged channel to the entrance of Chichester Yacht Basin is about 2 cables beyond; it is marked on the starboard hand by six green piles with triangle tops. Do not steer direct from Birdham beacon to the CYB beacon as this course crosses drying mud on the starboard hand. Steer to leave both Birdham and CYB beacons about half a cable to starboard and do not alter course to enter the dredged channel until two leading marks, BW perches with crosses on the shore on the port hand, come into line. Then follow their transit to the CYB beacon and follow the dredged channel.

If continuing up the Chichester Channel to Dell Quay, leave the transit when the CYB beacon is about ½ cable distant and steer for the green buoy off Copperas Point, leaving it to starboard. The channel dries only 1ft (0.3m) but is narrow and winding for the first 2 cables NE of the pile, so a stranger may not find the best water. Beyond Copperas Point the channel is shallower, drying about 4ft (1.2m) CD, thus having no more than 2ft (0.6m) at LW neaps. In the reach between Copperas Point and Dell Quay there are four barrel buoys to mark the narrow winding course. The first and last are red port hand, and the two between are green starboard hand, although when rusty they can be mistaken for red. After passing the last buoy the best water lies towards the end of the quay.

Thorney Channel

In this channel there is 6ft (1.8m) and more in most parts to within ¼ mile of the junction of the two creeks at its head. The entrance lies to the south-west of the south cardinal Camber beacon, which leave about ½ cable to starboard when entering the channel. The area in the vicinity northward of the buoy has been getting shallower of recent years, so do not try short cuts. An orange racing buoy is often moored near the Camber beacon. On the SE side of Pilsey Island on the port hand is a line of broken piles marked near its end by a red beacon (see photograph) which should be left close to port. On the opposite side of the channel there is the end of the similar line of broken piles to Cobnor, previously referred to. At the end of this is a dangerous shoal which dries out 5ft (1.5m) on which there is usually (but not always) a green perch and must be left to starboard. About 3 cables farther up the channel, east of Longmere Point, there are similar lines of broken piles on each side. The narrow fairway between them is marked by an iron beacon with red can top on the port hand side and a green beacon with triangle top to starboard. From here the channel runs northward and is marked by occasional perches, but note the 4ft (1.2m) shoal on the E side off the entrance to Crake Rythe SE of West Thorney.

At West Thorney there is the Thorney Island SC, RAF, and a hard. A number of yachts and small craft lie on moorings in this part of the channel. Thorney Channel divides at its end into two little creeks which run up to Nutbourne and Prinstead villages. Larger vessels should not proceed beyond the junction without local knowledge.

On Thorney Island there is a small village with a church, the sailing club, and a farm, but no shops nor facilities. Most of Thorney Island is RAF property and there is no access by road from the mainland to the hard, club and church, except by permission. There is plenty of room to anchor in Thorney Channel, and shallow draft boats and dinghies can go up on the tide to Prinstead where there is a boatyard: T. H. Payne.

Pilsey Island is uninhabited, and is little more than a semi-circular sea wall. For conservation reasons, landing is restricted to the beach adjacent to the anchorage (east of the island) during daylight hours and from 1st April to 31st October.

14.9. (Left) Port hand beacon off Pilsea (Right) Two beacons off Longmere Point marking lines of broken piles on each side of the Thorney Channel.

Bosham Channel

One of the most picturesque parts of Chichester Harbour is at Bosham, and the channel is easy to navigate though there are many yachts moored there, leaving a rather narrow fairway. The entrance of the creek runs in a northerly direction out of the main Chichester Channel half a mile west of Itchenor. The south cardinal Deep End beacon (unlit) marks the north east of the entrance, and it is best to keep fairly near this, giving Cobnor point on the port hand a wide berth. The first reach runs north and the channel is clearly marked by the numerous moorings.

The creek is a fathom (1.8m) deep or over until within about ¼ mile from the village, when it shallows and almost dries out a cable from Bosham Quay. Beyond this, Chidham hard, on the west side, extends three-quarters of the way across the creek, and it is mostly submerged at high tide; a post marks its eastern extremity and there is also a hard on the Bosham side. Above the narrows there is a narrow channel but at high water it forms quite a wide lake.

Moorings, Anchorages and Facilities

The Harbour Master (Capt Ian Mackay RN) controls all the moorings which are rented to yacht owners and for which there is a waiting list. His office is at Itchenor Hard, facing the river (Tel: Birdham 512301) where there is a Port Operation and Information Service, VHF

14.10. Deep End beacon at the entrance to Bosham channel.

watch is kept on Channels 16 and 14, 0900-1300 hrs and 1400-1730 hrs on week days: 0900-1300 hrs only on Saturdays during the season. Call CHICHESTER on Channel 14.

There are 6 white visitors moorings at Itchenor; each will take six craft rafted up.

At **Birdham Pool** there is access to the approach channel about 3 hours either side of HW depending on draft, and the lock gates can be opened 2 hours each side of high water with free flow in the lock for 1 hour at springs. At the **Chichester Yacht Basin**, 2 cables farther on, the river outside dries at CD, but in the channel dredged through the mud to the entrance there is about 3ft LW on an ordinary spring tide and more at LW neaps. Yachts may secure to the beacon piles or to piles either side of the lock gates while waiting entry. The lock gates to the basin can be opened at any time and there is free flow for 1 hour springs or 4 to 5 hours neaps. Lock control is indicated by boards: red (wait), green (enter) by day; at night the boards are floodlit and only when there is free flow a Q amber light is exhibited on top of the lock tower.

Anchorages. West of Fairway buoy on the south side of the channel: east of Pilsey Island: north of East Head: north of Sandy Point, at the entrance to Emsworth Channel.

The Itchenor Ferry. This useful service operates from the Itchenor jetty to: Bosham Quay: Bosham Smugglers Lane: or to moorings from Deep End to Birdham: 1000-1800 hrs on every even hour. Details from the Harbour Office at which other ferry trips can sometimes be arranged.

14.11. Itchenor hard and the Harbour Master's pontoon. Visitors' mooring in the foreground.

Facilities. At Itchenor there are excellent facilities as it is the home port of cruising yachts of all kinds and is a notable dinghy and small class racing centre, based on the very active Itchenor SC. Yacht yards include, G. Haines and Sons, H. C. Darley and Sons (also chandlery and fuel). E. Bailey, marine engineers, also supply fuel. Launching site at hard. Water at the jetty.

At the picturesque Dell Quay there is the sailing club, Ted Bailey & Co (Dell Quay) Ltd, Wyche Marine Ltd, an inn with restaurant, and 20 minutes walk to shops and garage. It is possible to dry out alongside the end of the quay on hard bottom, but mud on N and S of quay. Public hard north of quay. Moorings for shoal draft craft may be available on application at yacht yards but they all dry out. It may be of interest to add that in the late Roman era the Fishbourne Channel was much deeper and big ships came right up to Fishbourne, a mile west of Chichester. The excavations of the palace of the British vassal king, consisting of a rectangle round a courtyard, reconstructed gardens and quays where the ships tied up, are open to the public.

Bosham also caters well for yachtsmen. It is possible for a yacht to dry out alongside the quay (by permission of the Quay Master, Mr McQuail) where there is the Bosham SC. Launching site at quay or street end. Several yacht and boatyards including Burne's Shipyard Ltd, who also supply water, fuel and chandlery, and E. M. Coombes who is in Furzefield Creek, opposite Itchenor. Water at Bosham quay. In the village there are shops and a PO. EC Thursday. Buses to Chichester and Portsmouth.

14.13. Bosham Quay.

14.12. (Left) Verner beacon half way up the Emsworth Channel, and (right) Marker beacon just off Marker Point in the Emsworth Channel.

THE EMSWORTH CHANNEL

The Emsworth Channel is a straight, broad, deep, well marked fairway as far as its junction with Sweare Deep and, with sufficient rise of tide, it continues navigable up to Emsworth, where there is a yacht harbour and excellent facilities. With the aid of the lights referred to below, navigation is now possible at night under suitable conditions.

The channel is entered between Sandy Point and the Fishery buoy (Q (6) + LFl 15s). A line of yachts on moorings will lie on the port hand and to starboard the green NW Pilsey buoy (Fl G 5s). The next mark is the green N Pilsey buoy, followed on the port hand by the red can buoy marking the entrance to Mill Rythe. Three cables north of this and also on the port hand is Verner beacon (Fl R 10s). A further six cables takes one to Marker Point and the Marker beacon (Fl (2) G 10s).

About ¾ mile beyond Marker Point is the junction where Sweare Deep joins the main channel to Emsworth. Between the two channels lies a large expanse of mud flats intersected by creeks and covered at HW except for the small Fowley Island, which is little more than two disused salterns surmounted by a sea wall.

On the port hand the NE Hayling beacon (Fl (2) R 10s) marks the bend to the north west of Sweare Deep. A little further north and marking the middle ground of the junction of the two

14.14. Emsworth Beacon is a south cardinal mark (Q(6) + L Fl 15s). The channel is between the lines of yachts.

14.15. Fisherman beacon on the middle ground where the Emsworth Channel divides near Fowley Island.

channels is the south cardinal Emsworth Beacon (*Q (6) + L Fl 15s*). This prominent beacon is at the end of a line of pile moorings or trots along the west side of the Emsworth channel (see photograph). The Emsworth Beacon also carries a tide guage indicating the depth of water over the sill at the Yacht Harbour. The fairway is clearly indicated by the moorings. About five cables further up from the Emsworth Beacon is Fisherman's Beacon (*Fl (3) R 10s*). This is almost abreast of Fowley Island and marks the junction of three narrow creeks. The one on the port hand is Fowley Rythe and has 4 to 2ft (1.2 to 0.6m) CD, for a short distance, in which there are yachts on moorings. The starboard hand creek is Little Deep, and has at least 3ft for nearly 2 cables on ordinary tides at LW, with moorings for local yachts of light draft.

The principal creek between the two continues up to Emsworth. It becomes narrow and shallow and runs almost parallel to Fishermans' Walk, a long hard over the mud from Emsworth almost to Fowley Rythe which dries about 2 hours either side of LW, and has a notice board at its end. The channel is marked a further five cables on by Echo Beacon (*Fl (3) G 10s*). The wrecks that used to be a feature here have been removed. The creek divides again at Echo Beacon, the port hand creek leading to Emsworth quay and the other to Emsworth Yacht Harbour. The channel is very narrow but marked by perches. The sill at the entrance is 7ft (2.1m) so the depth above it at HW is approximately the Portsmouth height less 7ft. For example, if the Portsmouth tide table shows a tide of 14ft 2in (4.3m) there will be about 7ft 2in (2.2m) on the sill.

The following are creeks on the west side of the Emsworth Channel in order from the entrance:

Mengham Rythe: The entrance to this creek is north of Sandy Point and has an east Cardinal perch with tide gauge placed high on the mud flats on the starboard side. There is a bar at the entrance with only 1ft (0.3m) CD but within the creek there are pools with 4 to 8ft (1.2 to 2.4m) and even one of 20ft (6.0m). The channel is marked by perches but the yachts on moorings in the centre are the best guide to its direction. Less than 3 cables from the entrance there is a junction. The port hand creek dries out and leads to Eastoke and Sparkes boatyard (just west of Sandy Point) with a depth of about 9ft (2.7m) at HW but the main channel bears NW and continues to be 6 to 8ft (1.8 to 2.4m) deep until it bends to the SW after which it becomes very narrow and soon dries out. The upper reach is navigable by dinghies and craft of shoal draft and leads to Salterns Quay and Mengham Rythe Sailing Club, which has a week-end bar. There is a hard and boatyard and ½ mile distant is Mengham village, with PO, garage and shops.

Mill Rythe: The entrance to this creek lies about ¾ mile north of Mengham Rythe. It is marked on the south side by the red can Mill Rythe buoy which, as mentioned, is a port hand buoy for the main Emsworth Channel, and on the mud on the north side by an east Cardinal perch. The creek is marked by perches, red can tops port, green triangles starboard. For the first ¼ mile the bottom is uneven, and dries out 1ft (0.3m) at CD for a cable before deepening and widening with from 1 to 5ft (0.3 to 1.5m) as far as the remains of the pier at Wall Corner. It then dries out again and divides into two winding creeks, the northern one leading to Yachthaven and the southern to Hayling Yacht Co Ltd and A. E. Freezer Ltd, which can be reached with sufficient rise of tide. Facilities at yacht yards. PO, shop and bus stop ½ mile inland.

Sweare Deep: This wide channel runs from its junction with the Emsworth Channel in a NW direction between extensive mud banks. It is entered by leaving to port the NE Hayling beacon (*Fl (2) R 10s*). There is often a round orange racing buoy moored near the entrance. Sweare Deep has increased in significance since the opening of the Northney Marina and is clearly marked by the Sweare Deep Beacon (*Fl (3) R 10s*) five cables up on the port hand, and by the Northney beacon (*Fl (4) R 10s*) about three cables on at the entrance to the short dredged channel to the Marina. The channel is also marked by perches (red can to port; green triangle to starboard). There is a least depth of 4ft (1.2m) as far as the Sweare Deep Beacon and much of it is 6 to 8ft (1.8 to 2.4m). There are oyster beds on the starboard side of the channel with 'keep off' notices. Sweare Deep is well sheltered from SW winds and, although there are many moorings, it provides a good anchorage but rather remote from facilities.

Northney Marina. There is a dredged channel with a least depth of 1m (3½ft) from Northney Beacon (*Fl (4) R 10s*) into the marina basin, where there are berths for 250. Visitors are welcome and a vacant berth can usually be found. Call NORTHNEY MARINA on VHF channel M. Water and electricity on the pontoons, diesel fuel, restaurant, club, chandlery and comprehensive yard services. Northney Marina is the only marina in Chichester Harbour open at all states of the tide.

14.16. The channel to Langstone Bridge, showing two east cardinal perches (one has had a knock!), that are left to starboard.

Beyond this the channel divides into three, all of which dry out at CD. There are two east Cardinal perches on the middle grounds between the branches of the channel, two going north west, the main one west, and there is also often a round orange racing buoy in the channel between the perches.

The westerly arm leads to Langstone Bridge and thence to Langstone Harbour (see Langstone Channel page 117). When entering this channel leave the east cardinal perch to starboard and the line of small yachts on moorings to port. Once past the entrance to the channel the rest is easy, as although narrow and shallow it is well marked by perches, Near the bridge is the West Cuts west Cardinal beacon to be left to port when proceeding west.

The entrances to the two NW arms are separated by the more easterly of the two east cardinal perches already mentioned. These arms join again about 2 cables on where the middle ground is further marked by a west Cardinal perch. The channel then continues in a semi-circular bend to Langstone village and sailing club, and finally south to join the other arm near Langstone Bridge.

At Langstone village there is Langstone Sailing Club and The Ship Inn, with car park and public hard (launching site when room) adjacent at NE end of bridge. The hard on NW is leased to the sailing club. Buses to Havant and Hayling. There is a dinghy hard and park at Duckard Point on the south side of channel ¼ mile east of the bridge, where land reclamation is in progress.

Moorings, Anchorage and Facilities

Emsworth is an important yachting centre and there is anchorage in the Emsworth Channel and associated creeks anywhere clear of moorings, cables and the fishery areas (marked by notice boards on perches) mostly on the east bank of the channel. The Harbour Master's office is at Itchenor, and the whole of Chichester Harbour, including Emsworth, is centred under his

14.17. Northney Beacon (Fl (4) R (102)) and
the entrance to Northney Marina.

Authority. There are innumerable moorings within the area which are privately rented and application should be made to the harbour master or at the Yacht Harbour to ascertain whether any are temporarily vacant.

There are scrubbing piles at Emsworth, just off the sea wall and at Itchenor beside the hard: apply to the Harbour Master.

The principal base in the Emsworth Channel is the Emsworth Yacht Harbour. As stated, the approach channel dries out so that it can only be reached with sufficient rise of tide, but it provides 200 berths afloat alongside piers or to pontoons or piles for yachts ranging from 2ft (0.6m) to 7ft (2.1m) draft. The surroundings are not picturesque, but the facilities are exceptionally good and the charges moderate. Associated with the yacht harbour is a yacht yard, marine engineers, shop with chandlery, brokerage, car park, slipways, fueling jetty and water. Emsworth has all the usual facilities of a small town. EC Wednesday. Station and good bus service.

Appendices

Useful Telephone Numbers

Harbours where no local Custom's Office. Apply Southampton 29251, Cowes 2011 or Portsmouth 20055.

Ashlett Esso SC, Fawley 891764
  Creek Master, Fawley 848307
Beaulieu River Harbour Master, Buckler's Hard 200/234
  Yacht Harbour, Buckler's Hard 200
  R Southampton YC, Buckler's Hard 213
Bembridge Harbour Office, IoW 872828
  Berthing Master, IoW 872973
Cowes Harbour Master, IoW 293952
  HM Customs, IoW 293132
  Ancasta Marina. IoW 295724
  Cowes Marina, IoW 293983
  Medina Yacht Harbour, IoW 526733
  Island SC, IoW 296621
Chichester Harbour Master, Birdham 512301
  Birdham Shipyard (Marina), Birdham 512310
  Chichester Yacht Basin, Birdham 512731
  Emsworth Yacht Harbour, Emsworth 375211
  Bosham Quay Master, Bosham 573336
  Bosham SC, Bosham 572341
  Hayling Island SC, Hayling Island 463768
  Itchenor SC, Birdham 512400
Fareham & Portchester Portchester SC, Cosham 376375
  Fareham Sailing & Motor Boat Club, Fareham 280738
  Wicormarine Ltd., Fareham 273112
Hamble River Harbour Master, Locks Heath 6387
  HM Customs, Southampton 452007
  Hamble Point Marina, Southampton 452464
  Mercury Yacht Harbour, Southampton 452741
  Port Hamble Marina, Southampton 452741
  Swanwick Marina, Locks Heath 4261
  R Southern YC, Southampton 453271
Keyhaven River Warden, Lymington 45695
  Keyhaven YC, Lymington 42165
  West Solent Boatbuilders, Lymington 42080

Langstone Harbour Harbour Master, Hayling Island 463419
  Langstone Marina, Portsmouth 754820
  Locks SC, Portsmouth 829833
  Tudor SC, Portsmouth 662002
  Eastney Cruising Association, Portsmouth 734103
Lymington Harbour Master, Lymington 72014
  HM Customs, Lymington 74584
  Lymington Marina, Lymington 75444
  Lymington Yacht Haven, Lymington 77071
  R Lymington YC, Lymington 72677
  Lymington Town SC, Lymington 74514
Newtown River Berthing Master, Calbourne 424
Portsmouth Harbour Queen's Harbour Master, Portsmouth 822351, Ext 23344
  Berthing Office (Camber), Portsmouth 834764
  Berthing Office (Flathouse), Portsmouth 822916
  Camper & Nicholson's Marina, Gosport 542811
  Hardway SC, Gosport 581875
  R Albert YC, Portsmouth 825924
  R Naval Sailing Association, Portsmouth 823524
Southampton Ocean Village Marina, Southampton 229385
  Kemps Quay Marina, Southampton 32323
  Shamrock Quay Marina, Southampton 229461
  Weather Centre, Southampton 228844
  Recorded Forecast, Southampton 8091
  Marineline (Channel), Southampton 336161
  HM Customs (enquiries), Southampton 229944
Southampton Water Hythe Marina, Hythe 849263
  Esso SC (Ashlett Creek), Fawley 891764
Tichfield Haven Hill Head SC, Stubbington 664843
Wootton Creek R Victoria YC, IoW 882325
Yarmouth IoW Harbour Master, IoW 760321
  Harbour Office, IoW 760300
  R Solent YC, IoW 760256

Marinas in the Solent Area and Their Facilities

Marinas	Telephone Numbers	see page	All Tides	VHF Watch	Diesel	Petrol	Water	Electricity	Toilets	Showers	Laundrette	Bar/Food	Chandlery	Yard Repairs	Ice	Provisions
Lymington																
Lymington Marina	(0590) 75444		•		•	•	•	•	•							
Lymington Yacht Haven	(0590) 77071		•		•	•	•	•	•							
Beaulieu River																
Bucklers Hard Yacht Hbr	(059063) 234/200		•		•	•	•		•				•	•	•	
Medina River																
Ancasta Marina	(0983) 295724		•	•	•	•	•	•	•				•	•		
Cowes Marina	(0983) 293983		•	•	•	•	•	•	•	•	•	•	•	•	•	•
Medina Yacht Harbour	(0983) 562733		•	•	•	•	•	•	•	•	•	•	•		•	
Southampton																
Hythe Marina Village	(0703) 849263		•	•	•		•	•	•	Not yet completed	Not yet completed					•
Ocean Village Marina	(0703) 229385				•		•	•	•							
Shamrock Quay	(0703) 229461		•	•	•	•	•	•	•	•	•	•	•	•		
Kemp's Quay Marina	(0703) 32323		•		•		•	•	•	•	•					•
Town Quay Marina			Planned													
Hamble River																
Hamble Point Marina	(0703) 452464		•	•	•	•	•	•	•	•			•	•		
Port Hamble Marina	(0703) 452741		•	•	•	•	•	•	•	•			•	•		
Mercury Yacht Harbour	(0703) 452741		•	•	•	•	•	•	•	•			•	•		
Swanwick Marina	(04895) 6116		•	•	•	•	•	•	•	•			•	•		
Portsmouth Harbour																
Camper & Nicholson Marina	(0705) 524811		•		•	•	•	•	•				•	•		
Gosport Marina			Planned													
Port Solent			Under construction													
Bembridge																
Bembridge Marina	(0983) 847436						•	•								
Langstone Harbour																
Langstone Marina Village	(0705) 754895		Not yet completed													
Chichester Harbour																
Birdham Yacht Basin	(024)512310				•		•	•	•					•		
Chichester Yacht Basin	(0243) 512731			•	•		•	•	•			•	•	•		
Emsworth Yacht Harbour	(02434) 5211			•	•		•	•	•			•	•	•		•
Northney Marina	(0705) 466321		•	•	•		•	•	•				•	•		

Index

140